My Favour

A colourful collection of stories about horses. Dorian Williams, well known as a writer and BBC equestrian commentator, presents stories that are funny, sad, thrilling and spine-chilling among his fifteen favourites. A book to delight every horse-lover.

CINDY BEHZADI
1A2
R.om. 32.

My Favourite HORSE STORIES

edited by

Dorian Williams

Illustrated by Peter Kesteven

Beaver Books

First published in this collected form in 1968 by Lutterworth Press
Luke House, Farnham Road, Guildford, Surrey, England

This paperback edition published in 1976 by
The Hamlyn Publishing Group Limited
London · New York · Sydney · Toronto
Astronaut House, Feltham, Middlesex, England
Third impression 1983

ISBN 0 600 36232 9

Reproduced, printed and bound in Great Britain by
Cox & Wyman Limited, Reading
Set in Monotype Times Roman

Acknowledgements

The editor and the publishers are indebted to all those who have given permission for the use of material which is their copyright:

Michael Joseph Ltd, for 'Horses and People', from *Cobbler's Dream* by Monica Dickens.

Barrie & Jenkins, for 'The First Grand National', from *Grand National* by Con O'Leary.

Barrie & Jenkins, for 'Malek Adel', from *A Sportsman's Notebook* by Ivan Turgenev, translated by Charles and Natasha Hepburn.

Hodder & Stoughton Ltd, for 'Our Gymkhana', from *My Life and Horses* by Susan Chitty.

J. M. Dent & Sons Ltd, for 'The Smuggler's Leap', from *The Ingoldsby Legends* by Richard Harris Barham.

Michael Joseph Ltd, for 'Anything Long and Sharp', from *Flying Finish* by Dick Francis.

Michael Joseph Ltd, for 'A Ride at Sandown', from *Far From a Gentleman* by John Hislop.

Curtis Brown Ltd, for 'The Zebras', from *Adamastor* by Roy Campbell.

The Bodley Head, for 'The Old Firm', from *Brown Jack* by R. C. Lyle.

J. M. Dent & Sons Ltd, for 'The Invasion', from *War and Peace* by Leo Tolstoy.

Miss D. E. Collins, J. M. Dent & Sons Ltd, and A. P. Watt & Son, for 'The Donkey', from *The Wild Knight and Other Poems* by G. K. Chesterton.

J. M. Dent & Sons Ltd, for 'Point-to-Point', from *Pancho* by Dorian Williams.

J. M. Dent & Sons Ltd, for 'Mr Jorrocks at Newmarket', from *Jorrocks's Jaunts and Jollities* by R. S. Surtees.

J. A. Allen & Co. Ltd, for 'The Haunted Hunt', from *The Haunted Hunt* by R. J. Richardson.

Contents

Introduction

One of the enjoyable features of compiling a book of stories and extracts such as this is that one finds oneself reading and re-reading old and new friends in the literature of the horse.

It is, perhaps, not surprising that some of the greatest writers of all time have written about horses because until our own century horses were very much a part of everyone's life, and in addition so many people of artistic nature have found horses inspiring: hence the great paintings and sculptures featuring horses.

Some of the passages about horses that have appealed to me most of all have come in the works of authors not usually associated with horses. Tolstoy for instance, but what a vivid description of hunting occurs in *War and Peace*. Turgenev, too, may be a surprise, but he was a real countryman and the story here is taken from his *Sportsman's Notebook*.

They, of course, together with the immortal Surtees are the great classic writers: but who knows? perhaps some of the more contemporary authors will be considered classic in 100 years' time.

Monica Dickens is already established as a best seller – not surprisingly when one remembers that she is the granddaughter of Charles Dickens. And Dick Francis is now almost in the Bond class, his books having huge sales and being obviously film material.

One would expect his books to be expert, his having once been champion steeplechase jockey and jockey to the Queen Mother: but he is a real thriller writer and as such is now held in high esteem.

Like Dick Francis, Con O'Leary, John Hislop and R. C. Lyle have had distinguished careers as Racing journalists, and not surprisingly, therefore, their writing rings absolutely true, John Hislop's being also very amusing.

But most amusing of all in my collection is the gymkhana story from Susan Chitty's *My Life and Horses.*

The whole book is extremely funny, so much so that it was difficult to know which chapter to choose. Although she is lampooning the horsey set, it is obvious that she fully understands the problems of a girl groom.

I have been surprised to find how few people know the *Ingoldsby Legends*. I myself was brought up on them. I went to school in Thanet and remember vividly being taken to see the Smuggler's Leap. In fact I used to get my parents to take me every time they came to visit me.

In a way the very naïveté of its telling makes it all the more gripping. The real author of the Ingoldsby Legends was The Rev. Richard Barham who lived near Canterbury.

It is with some reluctance that I include a chapter from my own *Pancho*, but so much of my own philosophy regarding horses is summed up in this story that I feel it is justified.

In the foreword to *Pancho* I write that there is no such thing as a bad horse: a horse is as good or as bad as man makes it. Pancho himself is, of course, no longer alive, though I still remember him vividly. He had one of the most charming temperaments of any horse that I have ever known: yet I was given him as a runaway. With patience I steadied him enough to enjoy hunting him for five or six years, but he was always a handful. Why? Why should he be a runaway when basically he was so kind and gentle?

Despite every effort I never discovered the answer to that question, and so I made one up. Pancho is real, his story is fiction.

R. J. Richardson's story, 'The Haunted Hunt', is an old story re-told, brilliantly illustrated in its original edition: but how eerie it is: as exciting as 'The Smuggler's Leap'.

Finally the verse. Perhaps a poem about zebras should not really come in a collection of horse stories, but how charming Roy Campbell's sonnet is.

I only hope my readers will get as much pleasure from these as I have in rediscovering them.

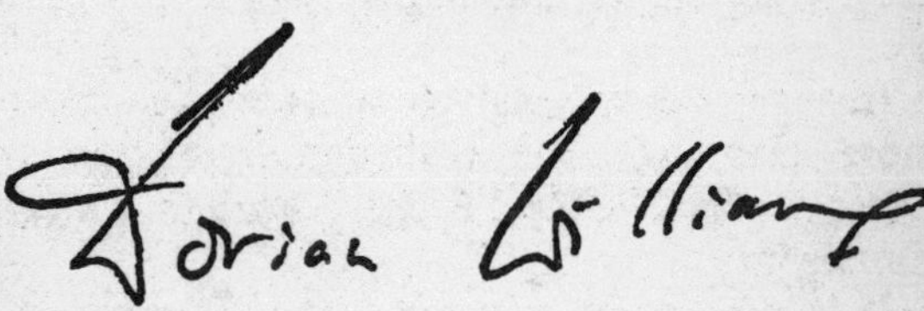

Chapter One

Horses and People

Monica Dickens

Black and bristling, the long patch of brushwood waited in the blossoming hedge, firm as a new toothbrush.

At either side, the small white flags moved gently against a colourless sky, and a lark went up, hovering his song.

The song disappeared in a surge of hoofs up the turf of the hill, and in a moment they were pouring over the jump like water, like waves rising to break, in a thunder of flung mud and curses. Then they were gone, bunched together for the downhill turn and fanning over the low bank on to the sticky plough.

A man with a black mud face climbed somehow back on to his wild-eyed circling horse, and galloped hopelessly after them. Behind him, the trim line of the new brushwood fence was torn and broken. A ragged bunch of twigs leaned out like a falling tooth.

A man in a raincoat and a long-legged girl in red

woollen stockings climbed through a gap in the hedge from the other side, and the boy who was holding the reins of the grey horse struggling on the ground shouted to them to get a vet.

Off to the left, beyond a white rail fence, most of the old horses had not even looked up as the surge and thunder of the race broke over the hilltop jump. The thin thoroughbred mare with the scarred chest had trotted the stiff stilts of her legs to the fence to gaze, head-up, long ears stretched, until the last hoofs had squelched away downhill. Then she dropped her head mildly to graze again, her ancient teeth pulling the grass bluntly up by the roots, so that she could only press out the sweetness and let the tift of turf fall.

None of the horses raised their heads when the shot cracked the damp air, and by the last race of the day, when the race was beginning, even the old racehorse did not look up as the dark wet horses crashed through what was left of the brushwood fence.

The point-to-point crowd were going home, wheels spinning in the creamed mud, jeeps bucketing past triumphant, boots slogging through the ruined car park, when Dora came to the gate of the top field and whistled. In the distance, round the side of the field, she could see the crawl of cars, congealing each time someone stuck in the gateway, and the last damp enthusiasts drifting back across the course.

It was the last meeting of the season. To-morrow the tents and ropes and flags would be taken down, the chestnut paling rolled. The cows would be back on the sour trodden grass where the crowds had milled and cast down betting tickets, and the farmer would harrow the patch of plough.

'Who won the last race?' Dora asked the spotted pony who was first into the fenced lane that led to the stable yard. The top of his rump was square, and his back flat as a table from years of his spangled ladies dancing on him and making pyramids. The pony checked her briefly for sugar and walked on, followed by the yellow Mongolian horse with a cow's high angular hips, and the faded black pit pony who sagged in the middle like a sprung sofa.

Ronnie Stryker, lounging at the yard gate in skin-tight jeans and cowboy boots, a match in his mouth for want of a cigarette, let them through one by one to walk across the cobbles to their own boxes. The horses who were already in banged on their doors and swung their heads about and made false ferocious faces of greed.

Slugger Jones and Uncle were taking round the feeds, Slugger concealed under a trenchcoat to his ankles and the Captain's old fishing hat turned down all round with a fly still in it, Uncle a goblin with a mealy sack across his bent shoulders.

'The last woman who saw you in that sack said she felt sorrier for you than for the horses,' the Captain told him.

'So she should be.' Uncle leered under his witch's nose. 'No one here now anyway.'

'Someone's coming in.'

Dozens of people went along the road past the farm every day, and some of them threw a remark, flippant, or soppy, or cynical, at the notice board arched over the gate, and a few of them stopped to see what was inside.

The Captain always let them in. Not for what they would put in the collection box. The year's harvest from the red and white box would not pay the water bill. It was for pride in his horses. And one day Roxanne would come. One day she would be on that road, going somewhere, coming from somewhere, and she would stop. She would have to stop, because the sign said Horses.

'We saw the sign,' the girl in red stockings told Dora, 'and I said to my friend: "How sweet," and made him stop. Home of Rest for Horses. "How sweet," I said.'

'Yes, it is sweet,' said Dora shortly. She was suspicious of girls who were tall and supple and looked good in the rain. She was busy, but the Captain was mixing a poultice in the saddle room that had no saddles, so she went with them along the boxes that lined three sides of the yard.

She showed them the gipsy's horse, with a hole where her eye used to be. She showed them the donkeys and the Shetlands and the roan horse from Ireland which had once lifted off a woman's church hat and eaten it. She showed them the brewery horse with the behind like a beer barrel, and she showed them the dusty brown mare who had been on her way to Buckingham Palace and never got there.

'A man was riding her from Cumberland to London with a petition for the Queen about common grazing rights,' she told them. 'But old Puss broke down a few miles from here, and the man went by bus.'

Most people asked why he had never come back for the horse, but the girl's mind did not work that way. She said, 'I prefer the trains myself,' and went on to the next loose box.

She looked over all the doors, clucking and chirping, but most of the horses had their tails turned and their heads in the manger. Spot came to lick her hand, and she fancied herself special. 'He likes me! They know, you see. They know when you—' She jerked her hand away as the old circus pony tried the edge of his teeth thoughtfully on the palm.

The man who was with her quickly put his hands into his raincoat pockets, but Dora said at the next door: 'Don't worry about Nigger. You couldn't get near his mouth.' She told them how he had come to them, a farmer's horse stolen out of a field, ridden all night by a gang of boys with a piece of wire in his mouth for a bridle, and left torn and bleeding in a gravel pit with half his tongue gone.

The girl looked sick, and the man licked his lips, as if he could feel the wire, and said nervously: 'Shouldn't he have been put away then?'

'He would have been,' Dora said, 'but we got him first.'

'At the races,' the girl said, 'there was a horse fell and broke its leg, right at the fence where we were, and they shot it. Wasn't that terrible? I wish I'd known about this place. They could have brought it here.'

'Not with a broken leg,' Dora said. 'Horses are too heavy. They can't mend.'

'I thought it was terrible.' The girl did not always register information. 'We were right there, you know. Right there, as close as I am to you. "How cruel," I kept saying. "The poor beautiful beast." And the man who had been riding it said: "Shut up. It's bad enough without that." He had one of those ever-so voices. You know. They don't care. Then when he took off his fancy red cap and wiped the mud off his face, I saw that he was only a very young boy really. And then, you know,' said the girl, with a faraway look in her eyes because it was an idea, 'I thought perhaps he did care.'

'If we go now,' the man said, 'we might make the Antelope for dinner.'

When it was dark, the old horses ruminated on hay, or stood thinking of nothing, like chickens, or dropped into the light, nervous sleep of an animal whose chief weapon is speed to escape. The pit pony was lying down, forelegs tucked under him, his eyes closed, nose resting lightly in the straw. The Weaver, who had carried Royalty on parade, rocked gently from foot to foot, swinging his gaunt bay head back and forth over his door. The two Shetland ponies stood head to tail, although there were no flies, and one of the donkeys lay flat out with his head under the manger, as if he were dead.

In other stables, the horses that had raced that day rested in bandages and expensive initialled rugs, the rain and sweat and mud groomed off them, the burrs and twigs brushed out of their splendid tails. The one that would not race again was a mound at the back of the slaughterer's shed. Under the stained tarpaulin a hoof stuck out, packed with a clod of turf from the hill.

Chapter Two

The First Grand National

Con O'Leary

The first Liverpool Steeplechase under Mr Lynn's auspices had been run on 29th February, 1836, but the race which is accepted in racing history as the first Grand National was that called the Grand Liverpool Steeplechase, in which seventeen horses competed on 26th February, 1839. Except for increasing the sweepstake for each horse entered to twenty sovereigns instead of ten, and abolishing the condition that the winner was to be sold for 300 sovereigns if demanded, the articles of the race which Captain Becher won on The Duke three years before on the same ground were not altered. The course was four miles, being twice round a two-mile circuit; the horses were to carry 12 st. each, and the owner of the winner was to receive the total sweepstake with 100 sovereigns added money. The winning owner was to return ten sovereigns towards the expenses. An attempt to curb ingenuity in evading the jumps across country is evident:

'No rider to open a gate or ride through a gateway, or more than 100 yards along any road, footpath, or driftway.' One article was much honoured in the breach: that which confined the race to gentlemen riders. No less than eight professional jockeys were put up, including two who were to become part of the Aintree tradition, though neither Jem Mason nor Tom Olliver had the imperishable fame of Captain Becher, who built himself an everlasting monument there by falling into a ditch.

If ever a man more than stooped to conquer, or rather tumbled into immortality, it was Captain Becher. It was said of Sarah Bernhardt – not she who ran in the foggy Grand National of 1895 – that no actress could die more beautifully, and in respect to the shade of Conrad's rider it must be conceded that no jockey could more impressively fall. In number the old master Assheton-Smith would no doubt outcropper him, for did he not take five falls in a morning's run and 100 in one hunting season, and does he not come down to us assuring the talebearer after dinner, firmly enough seated then, that no country was too high if you knew how to fall? But it is a later Assheton-Smith who is remembered for his Grand National fame: the owner of Jerry M., and he took the name on coming into the estates long after he had owned Cloister as Mr Charles Duff. But the name of the other tumbler, Becher, is literally fenced with tradition and is more widely known to us than to his contemporaries, but do not forget that there are more of us than of them; for he was a man of great visibility in his time, and in many of the old racing prints he was depicted in the act of falling. In 1831 at St Albans his horse fell on the flat when they were only a few yards from the winning post, and in the following year when the captain was unseated at the third fence he sprinted after the escaping mare across a field and, leaping into the saddle, was soon upsides with his horses and finished third. Alken, the racing painter, depicted him falling into a brook in the Leicestershire Steeplechase, which took place before the episode of the christening of the brook at Aintree, by which time he must have fulfilled old Assheton-Smith's secret of coping with difficult country. When the horse it was that died the artist gave Becher a look so mournful, as the survivor gazing on the dead in the shadow of a fence, that Valentine Maher said the picture shouldn't be looked at early in the morning and never on losing days.

According to his father he was 'broke to the saddle from his cradle'. Old Becher, or 'the last of the leather breeches' as he was called, was a horse dealer who farmed some land in Norfolk, and he forbade the boy to ride a donkey, as he said if he rode a donkey well he would never be able to ride anything else. But he learned to school his father's horses that were being turned into the shape of hunters, and he pleased one of the patrons so well that he left the stables for the Army, with an appointment in the Storemaster-General's department. It was while he was serving abroad that the Duke of Buckingham conferred on him the courtesy title of captain. When he came home he went back to his old love, and often stayed with Tom Coleman at St Albans, riding his horses. Tom gave him his first mount in a race at Hounslow. He walked with a limp from one of his many falls, but it must not be inferred that these were due to any defect of horsemanship, for the sport was in its infancy and falls were frequent, with imperfectly trained horses, often rejected from the flat for the steeplechase, which was disapproved of by many hunting men who would be then considered of the old school, and only just tolerated but not officially recognised by the flat racing authority. He had a thick curled beard that was said to increase appreciably his weight in the saddle. He slept on horseback or in post-chaises, travelling from one race meeting to another. When he fell it was expected of him that he would not only get up again but play a part in the finish, for he excelled in catching the others napping, and his guiding principle was that a race was never lost until it had been won. He was always ready to oblige the company with a song even at the end of a bad day. There are other racing men who sing when defeated, but their song is not meant for articulate understanding.

The first Grand National was remarkable for the association of a horse and jockey that was to continue for the first five years in the history of the race. The story of Lottery opens on the Jackson farm at Thirsk, where a mare, Parthenia, was put to a sire reputed to be descended from Eclipse and who was the original Lottery. The brown leggy foal who was narrow and short in the quarters was first called Chance, and when he was offered as a hunter at Horncastle Fair, John Elmore alone among the dealers took notice of him. He asked that Chance should be trotted up and down and put to jumping a rail, after which trial he bought the colt from Jackson for £120. At the first attempt to school him at Elmore's farm near Harrow he fell over a gate and was put out of action for some time. But whatever fate works to mingle the careers of jockeys and horses was moving to begin the story that would identify the names of Jem

Mason and Lottery – for the brown colt won fame after he had assumed his sire's name – immortally in the history of racing.

Jem was the son of a Stilton horse jobber, and when his father removed to Harrow he rode his cob there from the old home in a day. He schooled horses for Tilbury, a big horse dealer, whose Dove House Farm adjoined the Mason's land. But there was mettle more attractive at John Elmore's farm which was only four miles away. There was the pretty daughter of the house, and Jem's dreams of becoming a famous jockey were connected with his master's daughter. The rewards of success were to include for him that most cherished prize of all. One cannot attempt cleverness and say that he loved Lottery better, for the horse kept up a feud against him since the schooling days, and it was necessary for Mason to conceal his racing jacket under his coat until he was mounted. Then he took off his coat and the champion was sufficiently kidded to move tractably. Old training methods were severe, and the phrase of the time – 'horse breaker' – has a sinister ring; part of Jem's schooling culture was to arrange that the horse would have so unpleasant a knock when he fell that, remembering it ever afterwards, he would jump clean. Perhaps this explains why Lottery could not stand the sight of him, though responding with all his gallant spirit to those hands of magic and that guiding embrace, combined with the hypnotic power in the soul of all great jockeys, once he had slipped his coat off behind Lottery's ears and sat ready for the fray in John Elmore's blue jacket and black cap.

Jem set the fashion of the horsey dandy. His clothes were made for him free by a tailor in Savile Row, and here he could boast with the young men-about-town that he never paid tailors' bills. If Jem also evaded bootmakers' bills he had horse-and-jockey sense indeed, as he had the tops and bottoms of his riding boots made by two different firms in the West End.

The activity of his mind was such that he trained Lottery like a performing horse, making him jump over garden chairs and tables set for an alfresco meal; as well as the influence of the road circus we suspect here the breaker's pride in his finished horse, who had been judged a chancy jumper when Jem rode him a season to the staghounds. The fact was that he seemed to know his own capacity, and when he refused to jump and Jem insisted on his having a try, they were likely to fall. When he was competing in small professional meetings in the outskirts of London he bolted off the course at Finchley and, like the Playboy's mount 'kickin' the stars', made a tremendous leap across a lane. Though he fell it was apparent that Lottery was no ordinary racing hunter. After he had competed without success at the indoor Bayswater Hippodrome and run a dead heat in a steeplechase at Kensal New Town, his saddle slipped in the St Albans Steeplechase of 1837, for which Prince Paul Esterhazy had given Coleman a gold cup worth 100 guineas. The Prince, with Count Waldstein and Lord Claude Hamilton, watched the race, and the unsuccessful competitors included Conrad and Jerry who, with Lottery, were to become part of the Aintree tradition. Though Lottery had gone amiss before the St Albans Steeplechase of 1838, and was bled in accordance with the veterinary treatment of the time on the Sunday before the race, he held the lead until the last field, and finished third, being placed second on an objection. Jem Mason said that if Lottery had been at his best they would have won easily.

Tom Ferguson, who was the leading Irish owner of chasers, brought his three best to contend for the first Grand National, the prize, with fifty acceptances and the added money, amounting to £1300. Mr Ferguson himself rode Daxon, and he put up Byrne on Barkston and Mr William McDonough on Rust. Alan McDonough, who was a gentleman rider of high reputation, had the mount on Lord MacDonald's famous racing mare The Nun, and the professional Hardy was on Mr Vevers's Charity. Tom Olliver rode Sir George Mostyn's Seventy Four, Barker was on True Blue, and Mr Martin on Paulina. The other starters were Dictator, Conrad, Railroad, Rambler, Pioneer, Cannon Ball, Cramp and Jack.

Croxteth, Knowsley, and other country houses had parties for the race. Advance betting took place at the 'Talbot Hotel'. People were on the roads for Aintree from 9 o'clock in the morning, the start being timed for one in the afternoon. After the battle of Waterloo some Cossacks who visited England wore short boots and loose 'trowsers', and these were generally adopted in the dress of Englishmen, who then also began to wear frock coats. The three-cornered gold-lace hat had gone out with the French Revolution, and every man at Aintree had his tall hat with slightly curved brim, to be truly in fashion. Men of the people, who were already in love with racing that would become to their descendants a passion, had their top-hats but still clung to the knee-breeches and Hessian boots. The prints show several ladies in the excited crowd watching the finish on primitive stands and by the rails – the only rails – from the last hurdle to a winning post held by the judge standing at ease. These pioneers of the regiment of racing women wear large fan-shaped bonnets, shawls like cross-belts on a racing jacket, and skirts of majestic volume.

There would have been talk of the singer Josh Anderson's tip for the race at the theatre the night before. 'Will anybody lay me 100 to 10 Lottery?' he asked, after having disposed vocally of Napoleon with a 'kick from a Wellington at Waterloo'. Tips must have been plentiful on the road to Aintree: Charity, The Nun, Lottery, and the Irish pair, Rust and Daxon. No doubt there was a tip for every horse in the Grand National then, as now. A horse is thought to be invincible from the vantage-point of the training ground, but there will be ever so many invincibles at home going to Aintree with similar assurance of victory. But what else beside racing might the crowds have been discussing as they made that significant journey into racing history – going to see the first Grand National? The weather? It was a fine, clear spring day with just a trifle of wind from the Mersey to bring natural roses into the fair cheeks of Lancashire. The going? It would be deep and rough in the ploughlands, for it was a proper fill-dyke February, and a change from soft weather was wanted to enable the farmers to get on with the spring work. But these same were never satisfied; look at the way they and the landlords stood in the way of having the Corn Laws repealed, so keeping out the cheap corn from Poland, Germany and Russia in order to charge the poor people a whacking price for their own products. It was only ten years since no corn could be imported unless the price of English wheat rose to 80s. a quarter. How much better was it now when the home crops must fail and prices rise beyond all reason before those fine new steamships that could move against wind and tide could bring up the Mersey cheap food for the poor of Lancashire?

Wasn't Germany ruining the cotton trade? Corn was so cheap there that the mill-hands could live well on small wages and produce cheaper cotton to undersell Lancashire, so that instead of the Germans buying from Lancashire as in the good old times, they now made their own stockings and calicoes and threw the rest into the world market at a price that paid them but robbed Lancashire, thus taking the bread out of the people's mouths in every sense.

Anyhow it was a mercy that tea, coffee, beer, soap and candles were cheaper, and it was hoped we would get Indian tea, now that the Chinese were threatening to stop supplies sooner than compensate our opium traders. We had abolished slavery in our colonies six months ago, but these new Chartists said there would be slavery in England until every man should have the liberty of voting at the hustings even though he held no land or paid no rent, which was required by the new Reform Act. It gave Manchester and Birmingham their own Members of Parliament, though many on the road to Aintree had held with the Duke of Wellington, who was seventy this year, that the Act was not an end of the beginning, but the beginning of the end.

That was a bright name Captain Marshall gave his horse – Railroad – the new system of travelling that had become so fashionable since Liverpool and Manchester were connected by the permanent way. 'How different' writes Miss Julia Corner, historian, 'was the mode of travelling among our forefathers who lived in what are called the good old days of Queen Elizabeth; when country squires seldom thought of coming to London above once in the course of their lives; and a worthy citizen used to think it necessary to settle all his affairs, make his will, and take leave of his friends when about to undertake a journey to York. Were it possible for them to witness our present railroads, what would be their surprise to see a train of carriages flying along the roads, without horses, at the rate of twenty miles an hour? They would certainly think they were in some land of enchantment!' The surprise and the note of admiration are Miss Julia's.

It was nine months since Victoria was crowned, and no doubt some of the people at Aintree were choosing a consort for her during the long delay before the jockeys were all weighed out. There would be those to deplore the racy times at King William's court when he had rebuked an abstemious relative from abroad – Victoria's uncle it was – with the admonition: 'Nobody is allowed to drink water at my table'. At Ascot all the King's coachmen got drunk, except one, whose fate was as amazingly unkind as that of the early-morning worm, for it was he who was killed by a fall on the road home. No doubt he had his urn of postilion tears, for as the later cynosure of London society reflected in Reading gaol: 'Outcasts always mourn'.

Number boards were an invention that for some time yet were to lie behind the slow-parting curtains of futurity, and they would have been of little convenience to the eyes of the multitude who could not read. It was wise not to back a horse until you saw him going to the post, for you would not get the stake back that you had wagered on a non-runner. We can sense the atmosphere of the betting-ring from the contemporary one at Newmarket races described by R. S. Surtees:

'The legs (bookmakers) are scanning the list. At length one gives tongue. "What starts? Does Lord Eldon start?" "No, he don't," replies the owner. "Does Trick, by Catton?" "Yes, and Conolly rides – but mind, 3 lb. over." "Does John Bull?" "No, John's struck out." "Polly Hopkins does, so does Talleyrand, also O, Fy! out of Penitence. Beagle and Paradox also – and perhaps Pickpocket." '

The pencils are pulled from the betting books, but none of the layers likes to begin the shouting. At length a voice is heard offering to take 9 to 1 he names the winner. 'It's short odds, doing it cautiously.' 'I'll take eight, then,' he adds – 'sivin!' but no one bites.

' "What will anyone lay about Trick, by Catton?" inquires Jem Bland. "I'll lay 3 to 2 again him". "I'll take 2 to 1 – two ponies to one, and give you a suv for laying it." "Carn't," is the answer. "I'll do it, Jem," cries a voice. "No you won't," from Bland, not liking his customer. Now they are all at it, and what a hubbub there is! "I'll back the field – I'll lay –" "I'll bet – ponies – fifties – hundreds – 500 to 2." "What do you want, my Lord?" "Three to one against Trick, by Catton." "Carn't afford it – the odds really aren't that in the ring." Take two – 200 to 1." "No." "Crockford, you'll do it for me?" "Yes, my Lord. Twice over if you like. Done, done." "Do it again?" "No thank you." '

Then a man comes from the weighing-house where he

has been told that Trick, by Catton, 'don't start'. 'Impossible!' exclaim his backers. But the bearer of the bad news has been told by – himself. (Probably the owner, not the devil.)

' "Shame! Shame!" roar those who have backed him (it being a play or pay day), and "honour – rascals – rogues – thieves – robbery – swindle – turf-ruined" fly from tongue to tongue, but they are all speakers with never a speaker to cry "Order". Meanwhile the lads have galloped by on their hacks with the horses' clothes to the rubbing-house and the horses have actually started and are now visible in the distance sweeping over the open heath, apparently without guide or beacon.'

The first Grand National starts two hours late, for it is nearly 3 o'clock before all the seventeen jockeys have been weighed-out by the clerk of the scales in the weighing-house. There has been time for Lottery to come in from 9 to 1 to 5 to 1, and displace as favourite the Irish pair Rust and Daxon, who start respectively at 7 and 8 to 1. But all human eternities have an end, and at last those who have been diligently watching the line of horses and their gaily-coloured riders forming and re-forming at the angle of the course in front of the stables, no distance beyond the stone-wall and the grand stand, cry with throats of brass and lungs of leather: 'They're off!'

The coldly disgruntled who say it will be another false start are not listened to, for there is no doubt that Lord Sefton has lowered his starter's flag, and as there is nobody who can shout like the Irish, as the great Dr Cahill has been telling Liverpool, everybody knows that

Tom Ferguson has taken Daxon out in front and they have gone like the hop of a ball over the railed hawthorn before others have got up a gallop. But what are the Irish shouting about? There are four miles to go, with fifteen jumps on the first circuit and fourteen on the second, and now Captain Becher is coming up with Conrad, and the ploughland is knocking some of the shine out of Daxon's gallop – no, the race is not won yet – not by long chalks. Now they come to the railed fence with the 6 ft brook, and Daxon hits the top such a crack that it will sound for 100 years, but you can put your faith in God and an Irish hunter, and that part is true of Daxon, at that brook anyhow. While Daxon works an equine miracle in springing to safety, with the elegance of a performing horse at the end of a circus trick, Conrad has been too close for comfort, and Becher takes his best tumble into the brook. But Ferguson and Daxon have no advantage in ingenuity on the son of old leather breeches. A moment ago it might have been Daxon's brook, but now, and for ever until the last National chaser is forgotten, it is 'Becher's Brook'.

The captain felt the wind of Lottery's heels, and Rust, The Nun, Dictator, and Charity were leading the others, when he dived for safety into the deepest part of the brook, keeping down in his watery shelter until all danger of a brain-smashing cavalcade had gone with the leaping hoofs. But you know that the captain was not one who in self-pity would stay down, though uncommonly soaked in that christening of the Brook. It was not of fame or self that he was thinking as he pursued his horse and, catching up with him, leaped into the saddle, looking, we may suppose to labourers attired in smocks and corduroys in the fields, like a merman on the kelpie. The others having been delayed by plough and a deep wheat field, he caught up with them, and he was among the leaders at the next brook. But though Conrad was a great horse among the great, the contending pick of the country's chasers, and Jem Mason himself had ridden him in one of the St Albans Steeplechases, he was too exhausted or unstrung to cope with that awkward rail and brook after the sharp turn by the canal. It was no great fault that he crashed into the rail and slithered into the water, for many horses since that time who have escaped unscathed at Becher's have failed at Valentine's Brook because of that ugly turn, being unable to gather themselves from one fence to the next. Ninety years afterwards that fence before the brook was made virtually innocuous, as the crowded ordeal at the canal turn was judged to be too severe on the horses.

Now Conrad, picking himself out of the brook, takes care that the ambitious captain does not catch up with him again. The seeming phenomenon of riderless horses continuing to race is then a people's sight novel enough to be reported, and the early accounts, which leave so much to the imagination, will sometimes mention where these loose but game fellows come at the finish, if they keep going so long. Minus the weight and guidance of their jockeys they are a picturesque nuisance, though with some merit as a jumping performance, if in laziness they are apt to machicolate their fences. But when a horse goes on, the blame is not invariably his for leaving his jockey in the ditch.

Charity, who was supposed to be as familiar with stone as a bricklayer, because of her Gloucestershire training, was the only horse to fall at the stone-wall opposite the stand – perhaps it didn't seem a stone-wall to Charity, being less than 5 ft high. Meanwhile Rust had got trapped in a lane, the exit of which was closed by members of the crowd who did not want him to win, and Mr William McDonough's temper and blarney were equally ineffective in moving the gateholders to clear the way. Lottery raced up to Daxon on the second round, with Dictator, True Blue, Paulina and The Nun (who had been judged too fat in the paddock) going well enough to keep their backers vacillating between hope and fear. Dictator came down heavily at the first brook, and now jockey Carlin was up again; but the revival there was even shorter-lived than that of Becher and Conrad, for at the next fence Dictator fell dead. Thus passed the first martyr to Aintree, his saddle on his back, a St Albans worthy going till his last wind in the colours of Mr Oswell. Now Daxon, too, was down, and when The Nun failed to get the second brook after the puzzle of the canal turn it was seen that 'Black Tom' Olliver on Seventy Four, a dashing but too unlucky horse, had gone past Pioneer and Railroad and was catching up on True Blue and Mr Theobald's mare Paulina.

And now in a last call on 'Jorrocks's Jaunts and Jollities' we can say: 'Now all is tremor: silence stands breathless with expectation – all eyes riveted – the horses come within descrying distance – "beautiful!" three close together, two behind.'

But in the first Grand National there is one horse in the finish, and he is coming away to win on his own. Lottery is the word and Jem Mason is the man. It was said that they understood each other perfectly. Now is the fruitful fortune of all Jem's careful and rather stern tutoring of Elmore's performing horse, with the finishing gallops by trainer Dockery for a spell on Epsom Downs. Do not be jealous of Epsom's part in Lottery, Jem, or disdain to wipe your fashionable boots on the Downs, for no story of the Derby will gain more admiration than that of the finish of the first Grand National, when Lottery carried you 30 ft., forelegs to hind, in that record leap over the last of the three hurdles before the run-in. He won in a common canter, though not showing clean hoofs, after the ordeal of the ploughland, to Seventy Four and Paulina, True Blue and Railroad and Pioneer. All the others fell, except Rust, who, as the irrepressible punsters of the time must have said, was rusticated in the lane.

Chapter Three

Henry V, Act III, Scene 7

William Shakespeare

The Dauphin, the Constable of France, Lord Rambures and the Duke of Orleans are in a tent near Agincourt

Orl. You have an excellent armour; but let my horse have his due.

Con. It is the best horse of Europe.

Orl. Will it never be morning?

Dau. My Lord of Orleans, and my lord high constable, you talk of horse and armour?

Orl. You are as well provided of both as any prince in the world.

Dau. What a long night is this! I will not change my horse with any that treads but on four pasterns. Ca, ha! he bounds from the earth, as if his entrails were air; *le cheval volant*, the Pegasus, *qui a les narines de feu*! When I bestride him, I soar, I am a hawk: he trots the air; the earth sings when he touches it; the basest horn of his hoof is more musical than the pipe of Hermes.

Orl. He's of the colour of nutmeg.

Dau. And of the heat of the ginger. It is a beast for Perseus: he is pure air and fire; and the dull elements of earth and water never appear in him, but only in patient stillness while his rider mounts him: he is indeed a horse; and all other jades you may call beasts.

Con. Indeed, my lord, it is a most absolute and excellent horse.

Dau. It is the prince of palfreys; his neigh is like the bidding of a monarch, and his countenance enforces homage.

Orl. No more, cousin.

Dau. Nay, the man hath no wit that cannot, from the rising of the lark to the lodging of the lamb, vary deserved praise on my palfrey: it is a theme as fluent as the sea: turn the sands into eloquent tongues, and my horse is argument for them all: tis a subject for a sovereign to reason on, and for a sovereign's sovereign to ride on, and for the world, familiar to us and unknown, to lay apart their particular functions and wonder at him. I once writ a sonnet in his praise, and began thus: "Wonder of nature!" –

Orl. I have heard a sonnet begin so to one's mistress.

Dau. Then did they imitate that which I composed to my courser, for my horse is my mistress.

Ram. My lord constable, the armour that I saw in your tent to-night, are those stars or sun upon it?

Con. Stars, my lord.

Dau. Some of them will fall to-morrow, I hope.

Con. And yet my sky shall not want.

Dau. That may be, for you bear many superfluously, and 'twere more honour some were away.

Con. Even as your horse bears your praises; who would trot as well, were some of your brags dismounted.

Dau. Would I were able to load him with his desert! Will it never be day? I will trot to-morrow a mile, and my way shall be paved with English faces.

Con. I will not say so, for fear I should be faced out of my way: but I would it were morning; for I would fain be about the ears of the English.

Chapter Four

Malek Adel

Ivan Turgenev

A year passed, a whole year. There was not a whisper of news about Pantelei Eremeich. The cook died; even Perfishka was preparing to abandon the house and set off for the town, whither he was beckoned by a cousin, apprenticed to a barber – when suddenly it was rumoured abroad that the master was returning. The parish deacon had received a letter from Pantelei Eremeich himself, announcing his intended arrival at Bessonovo, and asking him to warn the servants so that they could make suitable arrangements for his reception. Perfishka understood these words to mean that he must wipe away some of the dust – though he had no great faith in the accuracy of the news; he had, however, to admit that the deacon had spoken the truth, when a few days later Pantelei Eremeich himself, in person, appeared in the courtyard of his house, mounted on Malek Adel.

Perfishka dashed to his master and, taking hold of

the stirrup, made as if to help him to dismount; but his master jumped down unaided, and, throwing a triumphant glance around, loudly exclaimed: 'I said that I would find Malek Adel – and find him I did, to the mortification of my enemies and of destiny itself.' Perfishka went and kissed his hand, but Chertopkhanov took no notice of his servant's attentions. Leading Malek Adel after him by the bridle, he strode off to the stable. Perfishka looked closely at his master – and had a shock. He thought: Oh, how thin and old he has got within the year – and how grim and stern his face has grown! You would suppose that Pantelei ought to have been glad he had found his own; and so he was, certainly . . . but all the same Perfishka had a shock: in fact he felt quite creepy. Chertopkhanov put the horse in his old stall, patted him gently on the quarters and said: 'Well, there you are, home again. Just look! . . .' The same day he engaged a reliable watchman – a peasant who had no taxes to pay – installed himself again in his rooms, and resumed his former life. . . .

Not quite his former life, however. But of this later.

The day after his return, Pantelei sent for Perfishka and, for want of anyone else to talk to, began to tell him, without of course losing the sense of his own dignity, and in a gruff bass voice, how he had managed to find Malek Adel. As he spoke, Chertopkhanov sat facing the window, smoking a long chibouk; Perfishka stood in the doorway, hands clasped behind his back and, looking respectfully at the back of his master's head, heard how after many vain attempts and excursions, Pantelei at length arrived at Romyon fair, by this time alone, since Leiba the Jew, from weakness of character, had not lasted out and had run away from him; how, on the fifth day, when getting ready to depart, he had taken a last turn along the rows of carts and suddenly, between three other horses tied to a post, he had seen – Malek Adel! How he recognised him at once – and how Malek Adel had recognised him too and started neighing and straining and tearing the ground with his hoof. 'And he wasn't with the Cossack,' continued Chertopkhanov, still without turning his head and in the same bass voice, 'but with a gipsy horse-coper; naturally I at once took hold of my horse and tried to get him back by force; but the beastly gipsy started howling as if he'd been scalded, all over the square, began swearing that he had bought the horse from another gipsy and wanted to produce witnesses. ... I spat and paid him his money: and may the devil fly with him! The great thing for me was that I had found my friend and set my soul at rest. Then, in the district of Karachevo, I ran into a Cossack who fitted the Jew's description – I took him for the thief and bashed his face in; but the Cossack turned out to be the son of a priest instead, and he took the skin off my back by way of damages – 120 roubles. Well, money can always be made – but the main thing is that I've got Malek Adel back. I'm happy now and I shall be able to enjoy peace and quiet. But for you, Porfiry, I have only one instruction: as soon as you see a Cossack about – which heaven forfend – that very second, without saying a word, run and bring me a gun, and I shall know all right what to do next!'

This was how Pantelei spoke to Perfishka; these were the words he spoke; but his heart was far from being as calm as he declared.

Alas! at the bottom of his heart he was not wholly

convinced that the horse he had brought back was really Malek Adel at all!

This was the beginning of a difficult time for Pantelei Eremeich. Peace and quiet was precisely what he enjoyed least of all. True, he had his good days, when the doubt which had dawned on him seemed to be nonsensical; he chased the absurd idea away like an importunate fly, he even laughed at himself; but he also had his bad days, when the nagging idea began again to gnaw and scratch at his heart, like a mouse under the floor-boards, and he suffered bitterly from secret pangs. During the memorable day when he found Malek Adel, Chertopkhanov had been conscious only of a blissful happiness. But the following morning when, underneath the low lean-to roof outside the inn, he started saddling up his discovery, after having spent the whole night by its side – for the first time he felt a certain pricking. . . . He merely shook his head – but the seed had been sown. During his journey home (which lasted a week) he had but few doubts; they grew stronger and clearer as soon as he returned to his own Bessonovo, as soon as he found himself on the spot where the earlier, indubitable Malek Adel had lived. . . . On the journey he had walked his horse for most of the way, swaying, looking from side to side, smoking his chibouk and without a thought in the world except occasionally to himself with a grin: 'The Chertopkhanovs always get their way! None of your nonsense for them!' But with his arrival home, another chapter began. He kept the whole thing to himself, of course; his pride alone would never have allowed him to speak of his inner anxiety. He would have 'torn in half' anybody who had even remotely hinted that the new Malek Adel was perhaps not the old one. He received congratulations on his 'happy find' from the few persons he happened to meet; but he didn't solicit these congratulations: more than ever he avoided people – a bad sign! He put Malek Adel, if I may express myself, through an almost continuous examination; he would ride off with him far away over the fields and set him a test; or else he would creep into the stable, lock the door behind him, and, standing right in front of the horse's head, would look him in the eyes and ask him in a whisper: 'Are you Malek Adel? Are you? Are you? . . .' Or else he would gaze at him in silence, with a fixed stare, for whole hours at a time, now joyfully murmuring, 'Yes! Yes! of course he is!' now perplexed and, indeed, troubled in his heart.

What troubled Chertopkhanov was not so much the physical dissimilarities between this Malek Adel and the other . . . of which, incidentally, there were a few: the other's tail and mane seemed to have been thinner, his ears sharper, his pasterns shorter and his eyes brighter – but this may have only seemed to be so; Chertopkhanov was troubled by what might be termed the moral dissimilarities. The other's habits were different, his bearing was not the same. For instance: the other Malek Adel used to look round and whinny gently, every time, the moment Chertopkhanov entered the stable, but this one went on munching hay unconcernedly – or else drowsing with lowered head. Neither of them moved when their master was dismounting, but the other came at once when called – while this one went on standing like a stump. The other galloped at the same speed as this one, but jumped higher and farther; this one had a freer motion in walking, but a jerkier trot – and was sometimes 'loose' with his hooves – that's to say, he knocked a back hoof on a fore one; the other had never shown such a fault – God forbid! This one, it seemed to Chertopkhanov, was always pricking his ears, in a stupid sort of way – quite the contrary to the other, who would cock one back and keep it there – watching his master! The other had only to see dirt around him and he would kick the walls of his box with his rear hoof: but this one never cared, you could have poured dung right up to his stomach. You had only to put the other one head to wind for him to be breathing at once with all his lungs and wide awake; but this one would simply whinny. The other was made uneasy by a rainy dampness in the air, this one didn't mind at all. This one was coarser, coarser by far! And he had none of the other's charm and a mouth as hard as – but why go on! The other horse was a dear . . . but this one . . .

These were the thoughts that sometimes passed through Chertopkhanov's mind, and they had a bitter taste. But at other times he would let his horse out at full gallop over a newly ploughed field, or make him jump down into the bottom of a hollow ravine and out again at the steepest way. His heart would faint within him from delight, a loud whoop would burst from his lips and he would know, know for sure, that the horse under him was the real, indubitable Malek Adel, for what other horse could have done the same?

Even so, however, there were frequent moments of pain and grief. Chertopkhanov's prolonged search for Malek Adel had cost him a lot of money; he no longer even thought of the Kostroma hounds, and he rode about the neighbourhood quite alone as before. Well, one morning, five versts away from Bessonovo, Chertopkhanov ran into the same princely hunting party, before which he had cut such a brilliant dash a year and a half before. It was fated to happen that way; as then, so again today – a hare jumping up from beneath a boundary fence under the hounds' noses and scuttling away across the slopes. After him, after him! The whole field went off at full tilt, and so did Chertopkhanov – only not with them, but 200 yds. to the side – exactly like the time before. An enormous ravine ran diagonally downhill and, getting deeper and narrower as it went, cut across Chertopkhanov's path. At the point where he would have to jump it, and where he had in fact jumped it a year and half before, it was still 8 yds. across and 14 ft deep. In anticipation of a triumph, so miraculously repeated, Chertopkhanov gave a victorious chuckle, shook his whip – the huntsmen were galloping too, but without taking their eyes off the daring rider – his horse flying like an arrow, here was the ravine right under his nose – over it, like the time before! . . .

But Malek Adel jibbed suddenly, wheeled to the left and galloped off along the brink, try as Chertopkhanov might to pull his head sideways towards the ravine. . . .

He had refused, or, in other words, he had not been sure of himself!

Then Chertopkhanov, blazing with shame and anger, practically in tears, let out the reins and drove his horse straight ahead and uphill, away, away from the huntsmen, anywhere so as not to hear them mocking him, anywhere so as to escape as soon as possible from their accursed gaze!

With lacerated flanks, and all bathed in soapy foam,

Malek Adel galloped home, and Chertopkhanov at once locked himself up in his room.

'No, he's not the same, he's not my friend! The other one would have broken his neck, but he would never have betrayed me!'

What finished Chertopkhanov off for good was the following incident.

One day, mounted on Malek Adel, he was picking his way through the priest's back yard, adjoining the church of the parish in which Bessonovo lay. With his fur hat rammed down over his eyes, slouching, with both hands dropped on the pommel of his saddle, he was moving slowly ahead; there was gloom and confusion in his heart. Suddenly someone called him.

He stopped his horse, raised his head and saw his correspondent, the deacon. With a brown three-cornered hat on his brown, pigtailed head, dressed in yellowish nankeen coat, girt well below the waist with a piece of blue stuff, this server at the altar had come out to inspect his plot of ground and, on catching sight of Pantelei Eremeich, thought it his duty to pay him his respects – and incidentally to get something out of him. As is well known, the clergy do not converse with secular people without some further purpose of this kind.

But Chertopkhanov had no time for the deacon; he hardly acknowledged his bow, and, muttering something between his teeth, was already waving his whip. . . .

'But what a wondrous horse you have!' the deacon hastened to add. 'It can indeed be accounted to you for honour. Verily, you are a man of wondrous spirit; a very lion!' The father deacon prided himself on his eloquence – and thus very much irritated the father priest, in whom the gift of words was not inborn and whose tongue even vodka failed to unloose. 'Having lost one beast, through the evil designs of the wicked,' continued the deacon, 'and no whit cast down by this, but trusting all the more in Divine Providence, you have taken unto yourself another, no whit worse than the former one, and perchance even better. Therefore . . .'

'What nonsense is this?' interrupted Chertopkhanov darkly. 'What other horse? This is the same one, this is Malek Adel. I found him. Rambling talk like that . . .'

'Eh! eh! eh! eh!' said the deacon deliberately, as if wishing to draw the words out, his fingers playing in his beard and his bright, eager eyes watching Chertopkhanov. 'How so, my good sir? Your horse, if God grants me to remember right, was stolen last year, two weeks after the feast of the Intercession, and it is now the end of November.'

'Well, what of it?'

The deacon went on playing with his fingers in his beard. 'It means that more than a year has passed since then, and yet your horse is now exactly as he was then, a grey roan; indeed he seems even darker in colour. How could that be? Grey horses turn much whiter in the course of a year.'

Chertopkhanov started. . . . It was as if a spear had been thrust into his heart. The deacon was right; of course a grey coat changes colour! How was it that such a simple fact had not occurred to him until then?

'You bundle of blasphemy! Leave me alone!' he barked out, his eyes flashing with fury – and vanished in a twinkling out of the astonished deacon's sight.

So it was all finished!

Really finished, broken right up, the last card trumped! Everything had collapsed at once with the single word 'whiter'!

Grey horses turn whiter.

Gallop, gallop, curse you! – but you will never be able to gallop away from that word!

Chertopkhanov rushed home and again locked himself up.

That this wretched nag was not Malek Adel, that between him and Malek Adel there was not the slightest resemblance, that everyone with the slightest sense was bound to see as much at first glance, that he, Pantelei Chertopkhanov, had been most grossly taken in, no! – that he had deliberately, and with premeditation, deceived himself, wrapped himself in this fog – of all that there could not be the slightest doubt! Chertopkhanov paced up and down his room: turning on his heels in the same way every time he came to a wall, like a beast in a cage. His pride suffered unbearably; but it was not only the pain of wounded pride that rent him: despair ruled him, hatred stifled him, the thirst for revenge blazed in him. But on whom? On whom was he to revenge himself? The Jew, Yaff, Masha, the deacon, the Cossack-thief, all the neighbours, the whole world, or, finally, himself? His mind grew confused. His last card had been trumped! (he liked this figure of speech). And he was again the most insignificant and despised of men, the most generally ridiculous, a tomfool, a blithering idiot, an object for the deacon's mirth! he imagined, he pictured clearly to himself, how that bundle of filth would tell the story of the grey horse and the stupid master. Oh, curse it all! . . . In vain Chertopkhanov strove to calm his raging bile, in vain he sought to assure himself that this . . . horse, even if not Malek Adel, was nevertheless . . . a good one, and could serve him for many years; simultaneously he would thrust this thought furiously from him, as if it contained a new cause of offence against the other Malek Adel, towards whom he already considered himself quite guilty enough. Yes, indeed! This jade, this nag, he had compared to Malek Adel, stone-blind oaf that he was! And as for the service which this nag could still give him . . . why, would he ever condescend to mount him? Not for anything in the world! Never. Sell him to a Tartar, as food for dogs – that was all he deserved. . . . Yes! That would be best of all!

For more than two hours Chertopkhanov wandered up and down his room.

'Perfishka,' he ordered suddenly. 'Go at once to the pot-house, fetch a gallon of vodka! D'you hear? A gallon, and be quick about it! I want the vodka standing here on my table this very second.'

The vodka was standing on Pantelei's table without delay, and he began to drink.

Anyone who then had observed Chertopkhanov, who could have witnessed the sullen fury with which he emptied glass after glass, would certainly have been horror-struck in spite of himself. Night had fallen; a greasy candle burned faintly on the table. Chertopkhanov had stopped pacing from corner to corner; he sat, all flushed, with glazed eyes which he would now lower to the floor, now turn fixedly towards the window; he would get up, pour out some vodka, drink it down, sit again, again fix his gaze on one spot, and remain stock-still – except that his breath came ever faster and his face grew ever more flushed. It seemed that within him some decision was ripening which troubled him, but to which he was gradually growing accustomed; the same thought came inexorably and incessantly nearer, the same image outlined itself more clearly before him, and in his heart, under the burning pressure of strong liquor, the irritation of wrath had already given way to a mood of brutal cruelty, and a sinister smile appeared on his lips.

'Well, anyway, it's time to act!' he said, in a business-like, almost bored tone of voice. 'Enough of this dallying!'

He drank down a final glass of vodka, brought out his pistol from under the bed – the same pistol with which he had fired at Masha – loaded it, put a few caps into his pocket 'against emergencies' – and set off for the stable.

The watchman came running up to him as he began to open the door, but he shouted at him: 'It's me, can't you see? Be off with you!' The watchman withdrew a little way. 'Be off to bed!' Chertopkhanov shouted at him again. 'There's nothing for you to guard here! This wonder horse, this treasure!' He went into the stable. Malek Adel, the false Malek Adel, was lying among the litter. Chertopkhanov kicked him and said: 'Get up, you crow!' Then he undid the halter from the manger, took off the blanket and threw it on the ground, and, roughly turning the obedient horse round in the stall, led him out into the yard and from the yard into the fields, to the utter amazement of the watchman, who was quite unable to understand where the master could be off to in the middle of the night leading an unbridled horse. He was naturally too much afraid to ask, but simply followed him with his eyes until he vanished round a turning of the track leading to the nearby forest.

Chertopkhanov walked with long strides, never halting and never looking back; Malek Adel – for so we will call him until the end – walked submissively after him. The night was fairly light; Chertopkhanov could distinguish the jagged outline of the forest, forming a solid black mass ahead of him. At the touch of the cool night air he would certainly have got drunk from the vodka, if . . . if it had not been for another, stronger intoxication which mastered his whole being. His head grew heavy, the blood drummed in his throat and ears; but he stepped out firmly and knew where he was going.

He had resolved to kill Malek Adel. He had thought of nothing else the whole day. Now he was resolved!

He went about his business, not exactly calmly, but confidently, without turning back, like a man obeying a sense of duty. It seemed to him a very simple affair: by doing away with the imposter, he would get even with 'them all', punish himself for his folly, put himself right with his real friend, and show the whole world (Chertopkhanov thought a great deal about 'the whole world') that he was not a man to be trifled with . . . But the main thing was that he would do away with himself along with the imposter, for what was there left to live for? How all this fell into place inside his head, and why it seemed to him so simple, would be difficult to explain, though not altogether impossible. Injured, lonely, without a human soul for friend, without a brass farthing, and also with his blood on fire from drink, he was in a condition bordering on madness; and there is no doubt that the most absurd actions of the insane have, in their own eyes, a special kind of logic and rightness; he never faltered, he was in a hurry to carry out his sentence on the guilty one, without, however, clearly explaining to himself exactly whom he meant by this term. . . . The truth was that he had not thought out what it was he intended to do. 'I must get it over, I must,' he assured himself dully and grimly: 'I must get it over!'

Meanwhile the innocent culprit jogged and ambled submissively behind his back. . . . In Chertopkhanov's heart, however, there was no pity.

Not far from the edge of the forest to which he had led his horse, ran a small ravine, half overgrown with oak bushes. Chertopkhanov went down into it. Malek Adel stumbled and nearly fell on top of him.

'Do you want to crush me, curse you?' shouted Chertopkhanov – and, as if in self-defence, he snatched the pistol from his pocket. He no longer felt any bitterness, but only the special feeling of woodenness that is supposed to come over a man who is about to commit some terrible crime. His own voice frightened him – so wild was its ring under the dark canopy of the branches, in the damp, rotten-smelling fustiness of the ravine in the forest! And then, in answer to his exclamation, some great bird suddenly began flapping about on the treetop above his head. Chertopkhanov started. It was as if he had woken up a witness to his deed – even in this dead place, where he should not have come upon a single living thing.

'Be off, you devil – away with you, to all the points of the compass!' he said between his teeth – and, letting go of Malek Adel's halter, struck him a swinging blow on the shoulder with the butt of his pistol. Malek Adel immediately turned back, scrambled out of the ravine . . . and fled. The sound of his hooves soon died away. A wind had arisen, which choked and hid every sound.

In his turn Chertopkhanov slowly made his way out of the ravine, reached the edge of the forest and trudged off on the road home. He was dissatisfied with himself; the heaviness which he had felt in his head and heart spread through all his limbs; he walked on, angry, morose, discontented, hungry, as if someone had injured him, robbed him of a prize, or of bread itself. . . .

His feelings were those of a suicide who has been prevented from carrying out his design.

Suddenly something touched him behind, between the shoulder blades. He looked round. Malek Adel was standing in the middle of the road. He had followed his master, had touched him with his muzzle, had reported his presence.

'Ah!' cried Chertopkhanov, 'you've come of your own accord, to meet your death! Very well, then!'

In the twinkling of an eye he had snatched out his pistol, cocked it, put the muzzle against Malek Adel's forehead and fired.

The poor horse shied to one side, reared up, jumped back about ten paces and suddenly crashed heavily down, wheezed, and rolled convulsively on the ground.

Chertopkhanov stopped his ears with his hands and ran off. His knees faltered beneath him. Drunkenness, anger, grim self-confidence – all had vanished in a flash. He was left with nothing but a feeling of shame and ugliness – and the consciousness, sure beyond a doubt, that this time he had made away with himself as well.

Chapter Five

Our Gymkhana

Susan Chitty

A week before Timothy was due home for the Easter holidays Angela had an idea. She had just jumped a pile of benches outside the Goose End cricket pavilion (strictly out of bounds) and perhaps that gave it her.

'Let's have a gymkhana!' she said.

'Our own, you mean?'

'With cups and rosettes and prize money.'

'But where?'

'We'll use the outdoor school. Max won't mind.'

I thought Max would mind but I was wrong. He seemed delighted by the idea and we fixed the date for Easter Monday.

'That gives us exactly thirteen days for sending out the schedules,' I said.

'We must have real silver cups,' chipped in Angela.

'And for ordering the rosettes.'

'There'll be a handy hunter class, of course.'

'And for finding someone to do the judging.'

'I'll make the handy hunter jumps,' said Angela, leading Tiddly Winks into his stall and not bothering to rub him down. 'And I'll think up a schedule,' she called, preparing for a vertical take-off on her racing bike. (I was glad she was too young for a car.) And that was all she did do. Everything else was left to me. I had to order the rosettes, make numbers for the riders to wear, raid Toothbrush's bamboo grove for bending canes, buy up the British Legion jumble stall for the obstacle-cum-fancy-dress race and type out the schedules forty times with one finger on Timothy's toy typewriter. Angela just had inspirations.

'What about a band?' she said. 'They always have bands. Do you think the Brigadier would parade the hounds? How about hiring field lavatories? And a judge's tent?'

In the end I told her to belt up and that we couldn't possibly afford all that unless she wanted to charge a 10s. entry fee for every class and as it was I'd had to substitute 1s. 6d hoof picks for silver cups.

'Hoof picks?' she screamed. 'But I've already got three.'

Timothy was half-enthusiastic when he arrived home for the holidays and heard about the gymkhana. He had made a glass-fronted rosette case in his carpentry class at school and he was dying to have something to put in it.

'Perhaps I could get a third in the fancy dress,' he said sadly. But Max had other ideas.

'Jumping practice this morning, Tim,' he said on the first morning of the holidays. 'You're for the red rosette in the juvenile jumping.' Gradually it dawned on me that the gymkhana was to wipe out the disgrace of Vodka's accident in the eyes of the Stillborn country in general and Toothbrush in particular. Max was most anxious that the Brinton-Farley children should be invited, presumably so that Timothy could beat them.

The rosettes didn't arrive until two days before the show. I had planned to make them myself but Max said he would pay to have them done properly. It was his idea to have 'Todd's Dressage Centre Gymkhana' printed on them in gold. Timothy sat unfolding them from their tissue paper for ages after breakfast and in the end I told him to take them up to his room and play with them there. He was out of the dining-room almost before I had said it. Later, when I went up to fetch him for jumping practice, I found he had pinned them all into his case in tidy rows according to colour. Judging from his performance that morning I didn't think he had much hope of keeping them there.

I'm sorry to say Easter Sunday was not a day of rest for me. I spent it collecting buckets for the potato race, spoons for the left-handed egg and spoon race, sacks for the sack race and obstacles for the obstacle race. The Colonel absolutely refused to have anything to do with the gymkhana. He was sulking because we were going to mess up 'his' school and 'his' jumps.

'Potatoes,' he said. 'Sex. What is this to do wiz horses?'

In the evening a tractor arrived pulling a load of junk. In a hip bath on top of some hen coops sat Angela.

'The handy hunter course,' she yelled. 'Someone unload.' Warren and My Man were run to earth in the kitchen. They handled the rusty oil cans, the school benches, the kitchen table with three legs and the wheelbarrow as if they bit. The field beside the school looked like a municipal dump by the time they had been dotted about it.

'Scare the pants off any self-respecting 'orse they would,' said My Man, dusting the rust off his boiler-suit.

'I hope so,' said Angela. It suddenly occurred to me she might have been practising. The Colonel had retired to his cottage with a bottle of Slivovitz or whatever Rumanians do retire with when they're really cross.

The gymkhana was due to start at two the next day but horses and, worse still, horse-boxes began to arrive before lunch. We had only sent schedules to local children selected by Angela for the badness of their ponies. But these were professional competitors who could scent a show at fifty miles, and arrive under power to clear every prize on the judge's table.

Angela turned up half an hour before the first event on a supercharged bag of bones she had scrounged from somewhere. She looked more ape-like than usual with her hunting bowler pulled over her nose.

'She shouldn't be here,' she shrieked, pointing her whip at a beautifully-turned-out girl putting the finishing touches to a thoroughbred. 'Castor's over fourteen hands.'

'Forget it,' I said. I was arranging papers on the judge's table in the teeth of the wind. We had economised on a judge's tent.

'Go on,' she said. 'Measure him.' The pony certainly did look tall and a dangerous red spot was appearing on each of Angela's mottled cheeks. I went indoors for a rule and could only find a tape-measure.

'Do you mind terribly?' I asked the owner of the thoroughbred.

'Please yourself,' she said, and went on talking to a friend. She was tall and had a Duke of Wellington nose and couldn't have helped looking superior even if she wasn't which she was.

I soon discovered that measuring a pony with a tape-measure is something that cannot be done single-handed by anybody except perhaps an orang-outang. Angela was now limbering up over a log at the far side of the field.

'I'm terribly sorry,' I stuttered to the back view of the Duke. 'Would you mind taking one end of the measure?' She interrupted a conversation about heavy duty tyres for horse-boxes, sighed and did as I asked.

I could have sighed too. With relief. Castor measured $56\frac{1}{2}$ in. at the shoulder. Fours into fifty-six go fourteen and half an inch to spare.

'I'm awfully sorry,' I said. 'But he's half an inch over the limit for the jumping class.'

'Shoes,' she said, pouring more scorn into the word than I thought it could hold. 'You've forgotten the shoes.' I looked at her blankly. 'B.H.S. Rule 999. It is usual to allow half an inch off the recorded height for the shoes.'

By now the children we had invited were starting to straggle up the drive on far from blood ponies. There was Cynthia on Muggles, Philida on Sooty, Amanda on Lollipop, Cordelia on Brandy, Emma on Tigger and Binary Fission's three little girls on their identical mouse-coloured ponies. Their parents arrived by car with their macs which was sensible because cloud shadows were chasing each other fast across the landscape. They stood around in groups shouting at each other the way people do on horsey occasions. Max and Milady (he carried a shooting-stick and she was in her Hardy Amies tweeds for the occasion) did their share of the shouting and so did a high proportion of the people who'd been at the fatal cocktail party. Loppy-lugs had come in a new Mini, a pea-soup-coloured one this time. Len arrived close behind her in a prehistoric forebear of the Ford Anglia. Handsome Odgson was with him. They went round giving people tips about the care of their ponies in the hope of tips of the other kind at Christmas.

Something brown and white and heavy snorted to a standstill in front of me while I was taking money from late entries. It was June B.F. on Marcellus.

'Octopus has twins,' she gasped. 'Girl twins. They arrived late last night.'

'Still it was Octopus,' she said. 'Eight legs, if you count arms.' There was no sign of May which didn't surprise me.

Daphne and the Mistake arrived in a Land-Rover as two-thirty struck. She had agreed to do the judging, with me as an assistant.

'Got a starter's whistle?' she said, glancing through the schedule. I hadn't thought of that.

'He'll do,' she said, bundling the Mistake back into the car. 'Just tap on the window.' I did, and the horn blew at once. The Mistake was well trained.

We had decided to have boring things like the leading-rein class and the best-turned-out rider first, then the jumping, then a tea interval for people to get into their fancy dress for the parade and finally the gymkhana events.

The first two classes went quite smoothly with Daphne standing in the middle of the school in the approved style and calling in the winners one at a time. The only trouble was that both classes took exactly twice as long as we had expected. I had no idea what a slow business it can be, signing on late entries, taking money, handing out numbers and shouting at people. I was glad Angela had insisted on hiring a loud hailer (a sort of transistorised megaphone.) I needed it even if Daphne didn't.

By the time we started the handy hunter class we were already an hour behind time. Luckily Angela's junk had been arranged beforehand in a cordoned-off area behind the judge's table. (We had decided not to use the school for jumping.) It looked really terrifying. The nursery fender flanked by deck chairs and the line of oil drums with flags on top were bad enough but the worst thing of all was the kitchen table surmounted by a line of washing. June on Marcellus was the first competitor and she, poor thing, had a clear round in the wrong sense of the word. Marcellus steered clear of absolutely everything and left the ring with his tail in the air to the accompaniment of a long-drawn-out hoot from the Mistake. (That was the signal for disqualification.)

The Duke of Wellington was the next to enter and she cleared the nursery fender, the oil drums and the wheelbarrow without a fault. But the line of washing lashed to a frenzy by a rain-bearing wind was too much for Castor's taut nerves. As he approached a particularly enormous pair of pink bloomers (contributed by Effie Symmons, the village layer-out) billowed at him. He went into a sideways skid, cleared the barrier with all legs but one and made off with a hundred yards of rope and several supports trailing behind him. The Duke remained composed but she had spoilt her round. Three more people didn't do much better and then it was Angela's turn.

The competition was not in fact against the clock, but I've never seen anyone go round a course faster. She entered at a canter but the bone-bag was in a flat gallop by the time she had cleared the fender and the wheelbarrows. Perhaps her idea was to get him round the course before he had time to realise what was happening. She took the corner after the hip bath so fast that the pony got his legs crossed and very nearly fell. I could see her face as she approached Beecher's washing-line and I must say it was frightening. I imagine a caveman might have looked like that just before sticking a stone axe into a dinosaur's jugular. And she cleared it.

A communal sigh went up as she tore out of the ring.

'Clear round!' June dashed up to her. 'Well done, Angela,' she cried. Unlike her father she was a good loser. But Timothy's father was now approaching the judge's table. His bull-like head was held low and he was a deeper shade of aubergine than usual.

'Timothy's in this,' he said. He meant the juvenile jumping which was the next event. He didn't say any more but he gave me a long bulging look and then planted his shooting-stick immediately behind my chair so that I could hear him breathing.

Another twenty minutes was lost while My Man (sportingly loaned for the afternoon) and Max's Man moved the junk and arranged Max's gaily-painted jumps in its place. Three of these had specially been ordered from a firm in Leicestershire and had only just arrived. Max hadn't been able to resist impressing such a large crowd.

The course was not terribly difficult and six people got clear rounds. To my amazement one of them was June Brinton-Farley and the other was Timothy. Timothy had put Tiddly Winks at the triple bar, wall and water jump as calmly as if they were ditches.

'He was given the needle too,' chuckled Max behind me. 'Hope it lasts for the jump-off.'

The jump-off was between the three Binary Fissions,

Emma, June and Timothy. All the jumps were put up a notch and we waited with baited breath as June scorched in. She seemed to have torn a leaf from Angela's book and Marcellus went round the ring looking more like a mini-war-horse than ever. Although he rapped the top of a triple bar it didn't fall. Emma had a refusal at the wall and the Binary Fissions all knocked bricks off it but Timothy had a second clear round.

'Keep your fingers crossed,' muttered Max. The House of Brinton-Farley was pitted against the House of Wisley in single combat at last.

The atmosphere was tense. All the jumps went up again and the double oxer (a brush fence in a cage of poles) looked really terrifying. June went in first. I could see Toothbrush's moustache quivering with nerves on the other side of the arena. She cleared the triple bar, the wall and the gate. You could only see the tips of Marcellus's ears as he approached the oxer and at the moment he should have taken off something funny happened to these. They stopped and disappeared altogether for several seconds. I thought he had refused but June must have done something to him that made him think better of it because quite suddenly he was in the air. But not for long enough. Instead of landing on the far side of the jump he landed clean in the middle of it. Poles and brushwood flew in all directions and June hung for several seconds on her pony's neck before joining them. Through the din of splitting and thudding wood I distinctly heard Max shout behind me 'Thank God.' As June and Marcellus picked their way out of the ruins of jump eight Daphne boomed 'Refusal, four faults. Failure to clear obstacle, four faults. Failure of rider to maintain contact with horse, four faults. Total twelve faults.'

Now it was Timothy's turn. A clear round, or even a moderately clear round, would win the hoof pick and the red rosette and save the family honour. He trotted into the ring wearing a calm, almost vacant expression. The Colonel had washed Tiddly Winks' tail in Omo that morning and she was carrying it vertically. I didn't get the feeling Timothy was driving her but she didn't need driving. Her short white ears were pointed and she really seemed to be enjoying herself. She'd already done half her third clear round when a most extraordinary thing happened. Timothy missed jump six. It was only a single bar and not particularly high but it was tucked away in a corner and required a detour.

'Number six,' yelled the crowd as a man, while a look of unspeakable joy began to spread over Toothbrush's normally gloomy mug. Max yelled again so loud I thought my ear drums would burst. 'Six, you unmentionable unmentionable.' But Timothy took no notice and cleared the remaining three jumps in perfect style. But to no avail. For in the jumping world it is better to have jumped and knocked everything flying than never to have jumped at all.

Max was at his side as soon as he left the ring. I had never seen his face such a dangerous colour before. 'Why the hell did you leave out number six?' he trumpeted. Timothy just yawned, dismounted and took a rather wavy line for the stables without even bothering to tie Tiddly Winks up first. Max was left flabbergasted.

The jumping for children of fourteen and over on ponies of fourteen hands and under was won by Angela after a hard-fought duel with the Duke and the rain began during the tea interval and did not improve the fancy dress parade. The girl who represented Lady

Godiva in a pink bathing costume and a nylon wig was all right but the boy who had covered himself and his pony in newspaper to represent Keeping Britain Tidy was not. I found it difficult to write on a pad which was also being rained on. Nobody's temper was improved by the fact that Angela won the bending, the potato and the left-handed egg and spoon race in quick succession.

'Why did it have to be left-handed?' said Cynthia who had come second. I hoped she wouldn't notice the hand with which Angela was signing on for the next race. It was not the right one.

By the time the ponies had squelched their way through the relay race they too were showing signs of annoyance. There was a good deal of kicking and squealing going on and one animal even forgot itself so far as to buck. Halfway through the obstacle race Cynthia, with mud on the seat of her jodhpurs, was brought to the judge's table in tears, and by the end of the pairs' race riders were dropping off like apples in a high wind.

'Call it a day,' said Daphne, looking at her watch. 'Even if there are four more events to come.' It was seven o'clock by then. Those who cared to stay were presented with their hoof picks by Milady through the rumpus-room window because of the weather. Angela got seven hoof picks but Timothy didn't show up to collect his second for jumping. I discovered why when I went to the hay loft to do evening feeds. (The Colonel had taken the evening off.) He was curled up there fast asleep. He didn't even wake when he was carried indoors, undressed and put into his own bed. It looked as if they had overdone the needle. Perhaps he got the dose that Tiddly Winks should have had.

Chapter Six

The Smuggler's Leap

A legend of Thanet

Richard Harris Barham

'Near this hamlet (Acol) is a long-disused chalkpit of formidable depth, known by the name of "The Smuggler's Leap". The tradition of the parish runs, that a riding-officer from Sandwich, called Anthony Gill, lost his life here in the early part of the present (18th) century, while in pursuit of a smuggler. A fog coming on, both parties went over the precipice. The smuggler's horse *only*, it is said, was found crushed beneath its rider. The spot has, of course been haunted ever since.' See *Supplement to Lewis's History of Thanet by the Rev. Samuel Pegge, A. M., Vicar of Gomersham.* W. Bristow, Canterbury, 1796, p. 127.

The fire-flash shines from Reculver cliff,
And the answering light burns blue in the skiff,
And there they stand
That smuggling band,

Some in the water and some on the sand,
Ready those contraband goods to land;
The night is dark, they are silent and still,
– At the head of the party is Smuggler Bill!

'Now lower away! come, lower away!
We must be far ere the dawn of the day.
If Exciseman Gill should get scent of the prey,
And should come, and should catch us here,
what would he say?
Come, lower away, lads – once on the hill,
We'll laugh, ho! ho! at Exciseman Gill!'

The cargo's lower'd from the dark skiff's side,
And the tow-line drags the tubs through the tide,
No trick nor flam,
But your real Schiedam.
'Now mount, my merry men, mount and ride!'
Three on the crupper and one before,
And the led-horse laden with five tubs more;
But the rich point-lace,
In the oil-skin case
Of proof to guard its contents from ill,
The 'prime of the swag', is with Smuggler Bill!

Merrily now in a goodly row,
Away and away those smugglers go,
And they laugh at Exciseman Gill, ho! ho!
When out from the turn
Of the road to Herne,
Comes Gill, wide awake to the whole concern!
Exciseman Gill, in all his pride,
With his custom-house officers all at his side!

– They were called custom-house officers then;
There were no such things as 'Preventive men'.
Sauve qui peut!
  That lawless crew,
Away, and away, and away they flew!
Some dropping one tub, some dropping two; –
Some gallop this way, and some gallop that,
Through Fordwich Level – o'er Sandwich Flat,
Some fly that way, and some fly this,
Like a covey of birds when the sportsmen miss,
  These in their hurry
  Make for Sturry,
With Custom-house officers close in their rear,
Down Rushbourne Lane, and so by Westbere,
  None of them stopping,
  But shooting and popping,
And many a Custom-house bullet goes slap
Through many a three-gallon tub like a tap
  And the gin spurts out
  And squirts all about,
And many a heart grew sad that day
That so much good liquor was so thrown away.

  Sauve qui peut!
  That lawless crew,
Away, and away, and away they flew!
Some seek Whitstable – some Grove Ferry,
Spurring and whipping like madmen – very –
For the life! for the life! they ride! they ride!
And the Custom-house officers all divide,
And they gallop on after them far and wide!
All, all, save one – Exciseman Gill –
He sticks to the skirts of Smuggler Bill!

Smuggler Bill is six feet high,
He has curling locks and a roving eye,
He has a tongue and he has a smile
Trained the female heart to beguile,
And there is not a farmer's wife in the Isle,
    From St Nicholas quite
    To the Foreland Light,
But that eye, and that tongue, and that smile
                                        will wheedle her
To have done with the Grocer and make *him*
                                        her Tea-dealer;
There is not a farmer there but he still
Buys gin and tobacco from Smuggler Bill.

Smuggler Bill rides gallant and gay
On his dapple-grey mare, away, and away,
And he pats her neck, and he seems to say,
'Follow who will, ride after who may,
    In sooth he had need
    Fodder his steed,
In lieu of Lent-corn, with a Quicksilver feed;
– Nor oats, nor beans, nor the best of old hay,
Will make him a match for my own dapple-grey!
Ho! ho! – ho! ho!' says Smuggler Bill –
He draws out a flask and he sips his fill,
And he laughs 'Ho! ho!' at Exciseman Gill.

Down Chislett Lane, so free and so fleet
Rides Smuggler Bill, and away to Up-street;
    Sarre Bridge is won –
    Bill thinks it fun;
'Ho! ho! the old tub-gauging son of a gun –
His wind will be thick, and his breeks be thin,
Ere a race like this he may hope to win!'

Away, away
Goes the fleet dapple-grey,
Fresh as the breeze, and free as the wind,
And Exciseman Gill lags far behind.
'I would give my soul,' quoth Exciseman Gill,
'For a nag that would catch that Smuggler Bill! –
No matter for blood, no matter for bone,
No matter for colour, bay, brown or roan,
So I had but one!'
A voice cried 'Done!'
'Aye, dun,' said Exciseman Gill, and he spied
A Custom-house officer close by his side,
On a high-trotting horse with a dun-coloured hide. –
'Devil take me,' again quoth Exciseman Gill,
'If I had but that horse, I'd have Smuggler Bill!'
From his using such shocking expressions, it's plain
That Exciseman Gill was rather profane. . . .
A sad old scoundrel as ever you knew,
And he rode in his stirrups sixteen stone two.
– He'd just uttered the words which I've mentioned to you,
When his horse coming slap on his knees with him, threw
Him head over heels, and away he flew,
And Exciseman Gill was bruised black and blue.
When he arose
His hands and his clothes
Were as filthy as could be, – he'd pitch'd on his nose,
And roll'd over and over again in the mud,
And his nose and his chin were all covered with blood;

Yet he screamed with passion, 'I'd rather *grill*
Than not come up with that Smuggler Bill!'
– 'Mount! Mount!' quoth the Custom-house officer, 'get
On the back of my Dun, you'll bother him yet.
Your words are plain, though they're somewhat rough,
"Done and Done" between gentlemen's always enough! –
I'll lend you a life – there – you're up on him – so
He's a rum one to look at – a devil to go!'
Exciseman Gill
Dash'd up the hill,
And mark'd not, so eager was he in pursuit,
The queer Custom-house officer's queer-looking boot.

Smuggler Bill rides on amain
He slacks not girth and he draws not rein,
Yet the dapple-grey mare bounds on in vain,
For nearer now – and he hears it plain –
Sounds the tramp of a horse – ''Tis the Gauger again!'

Smuggler Bill
Dashes round by the mill
That stands near the road upon Monkton Hill, –
'Now speed, – now speed,
My dapple-grey steed,
Thou ever, my dapple, wert good at need!
O'er Monkton Mead, and through Minster Level,
We'll baffle him yet, be he gauger or devil!
For Manston Cave, away! away!

Now speed thee, now speed thee, my good
dapple-grey,
It shall never be said that Smuggler Bill
Was run down like a hare by Exciseman Gill!'

Manston Cave was Bill's abode;
A mile to the north of the Ramsgate road,
(Of late they say
It's been taken away
That is levell'd, and filled up with chalk and clay
By a gentleman there of the name of Day),
Thither he urges his good dapple-grey;
And the dapple-grey steed,
Still good at need,
Though her chest it pants, and her flanks they
bleed,
Dashes along at the top of her speed;
But nearer and nearer Exciseman Gill
Cries 'Yield thee! now yield thee, thou
Smuggler Bill!'

Smuggler Bill, he looks behind,
And he sees a Dun horse come swift as the wind,
And his nostrils smoke and his eyes they blaze
Like a couple of lamps on a yellow post-chaise!
Every shoe he has got
Appears red-hot!
And sparks round his ears snap, crackle, and play,
And his tail cocks up in a very odd way,
Every hair in his mane seems a porcupine's quill,
And there on his back sits Exciseman Gill,
Crying, 'Yield thee! now yield thee, thou
Smuggler Bill!'

Smuggler Bill from his holster drew
A large horse-pistol of which he had two!
        Made by Nock;
        He pull'd back the cock
As far as he could to the back of the lock;
The trigger he touch'd, and the welkin rang
To the sound of the weapon, it made such a bang;
Smuggler Bill ne'er missed his aim,
The shot told true on the Dun – but there came
From the hole where it enter'd, – not blood, –
                                                        but flame!
        – He changed his plan
        And fired at the man;
But his second horse-pistol flashed in the pan!
And Exciseman Gill with a hearty good will,
Made a grab at the collar of Smuggler Bill.

The dapple-grey mare made a desperate bound
When that queer Dun horse on her flank she
                                                        found,
Alack! and alas! on what dangerous ground!
It's enough to make one's flesh to creep
To stand on that fearful verge, and peep
Down the rugged sides so dreadfully steep,
Where the chalk-hole yawns full sixty feet deep,
O'er which that steed took that desperate leap!
It was so dark then under the trees,
No horse in the world could tell chalk from cheese –
Down they went – o'er that terrible fall –
Horses, Exciseman, Smuggler and all!

        Below were found
        Next day on the ground

By an elderly gentleman walking his round,
(I wouldn't have seen such a sight for a pound),
All smash'd and dash'd, three mangled corses,
Two of them human – the third was a horse's –
That good dapple-grey, and Exciseman Gill
Yet grasping the collar of Smuggler Bill!
But where was the Dun? that terrible Dun?
From that terrible night he was seen by none! –
There are some people think, though I am not one,
That part of the story all nonsense and fun,
    But the country-folks there,
    One and all declare,
When the 'Crowner's Quest' came to sit on the pair,
They heard a loud Horse-laugh up in the air! –
    – If in one of the trips
    Of the steam-boat *Eclipse*
You should go down to Margate to look at the ships,
Or to take what the bathing-room people call 'Dips',
    You may hear old folks talk
    Of that quarry of chalk;
Or go over – it's rather too far for a walk,
But a three-shilling drive will give you a peep
At that fearful chalk-pit – so awfully deep,
Which is call'd to this moment 'The Smuggler's Leap!'
Nay more, I am told, on a moonshiny night,
If you're 'plucky', and not over-subject to fright,
And go and look over that chalk-pit white,
    You may see, if you will,
    The ghost of Old Gill
Grappling the Ghost of Smuggler Bill,

And the Ghost of the dapple-grey lying between
'em –
I'm told so – I can't say I know one who's seen
'em!

MORAL

And now, gentle Reader, one word ere we part,
Just take a friend's counsel, and lay it to heart.
Imprimis, don't smuggle! – if, bent to please
Beauty,
You must buy French lace, – purchase what has
paid duty.
Don't use naughty words, in the next place, –
and ne'er in
Your language adopt a bad habit of swearing!
Never say 'Devil take me!'
Or 'shake me!' – or 'bake me'
Or such-like expressions – remember Old Nick
To take folks at their word is remarkably quick.
Another sound maxim I'd wish you to keep,
Is, 'Mind what you are after, and – Look ere
you Leap!'

Above all, to my last gravest caution attend –
NEVER BORROW A HORSE YOU DON'T KNOW OF A
FRIEND ! ! !

Chapter Seven

Anything Long and Sharp

Dick Francis

The next afternoon I went on a flight to New York.

With Billy.

The ice between us was as cold as the rarefied air outside the pressurised stratocruiser which took us. Yardman, I reflected, wasn't showing much sense in pushing us off together so soon, and on a two-day journey at that.

The wide cold stare was somewhat marred by the blackish streaks and yellow smudges left by my fist, and Billy was distinctly warier than he had been on the French journeys. There were no elementary taunts this time; but at the end of everything he said to me he tacked on the words 'Lord Grey', and made them sound like an insult.

He tried nothing so crude as punching to make my trip memorable; instead he smashed down one of the metal bars as I was fixing a guy chain during the loading. I looked up angrily, squeezing four squashed right fingers in my left hand, and met his watchful waiting eyes. He was looking down at me with interest, with faintly sneering calculation, to see what I would do.

If anyone else had dropped the bar, I would have known it was accidental. With Billy, apart from the force with which it had landed, I knew it wasn't. But the day had barely begun, and the cargo was much too valuable to jeopardise for personal reasons, which I dare say he was counting on. When he saw that I was not going to retaliate, or at least not instantly, he nodded in satisfaction, picked up the bar with a small cold private smile, and calmly began putting it into place.

The loading was finished and the plane took off. There were thick dark red marks across my fingers an inch below the nails, and they throbbed all the way to America.

With us on that trip, looking after a full load of twelve horses, we took two other grooms, an elderly deaf one supplied by Yardman, and another man travelling privately with one particular horse. Owners occasionally sent their own grooms instead of entrusting their valued or difficult animals entirely to Yardman's, and far from resenting it I had learned from Timmie and Conker to be glad of the extra help.

The horse involved on this occasion had come from Norway, stayed in England overnight, and was bound for a racing stable in Virginia. The new owner had asked for the Norwegian groom to go all the way, at his expense, so that the horse should have continuous care on the journey. It didn't look worth it, I reflected, looking over at it idly while I checked the horses in the next box. A weak-necked listless chestnut, it had a straggle of hair round the fetlocks which suggested there had been a cart horse not far enough back in its ancestry, and the acute-angled hocks didn't have the best conformation for speed. Norway was hardly famed for the quality of its racing any more, even though it was possibly the Vikings who had invented the whole sport. They placed heaps of valued objects (the prizes) at varying distances from the starting point: then all the competitors lined up, and with wild whoops the race began. The prizes nearest the start were the smallest, the furthest away the richest, so each rider had to decide what suited his mount best, a quick sprint or a shot at stamina. Choosing wrong meant getting no prize at all. Twelve hundred years ago fast sturdy racing horses had been literally worth a fortune in Norway, but the smooth-skinned long-legged descendants of those tough shaggy ponies didn't count for much in the modern thoroughbred industry. It was sentiment, I supposed, which caused an American to pay for such an inferior-looking animal to travel so far from home.

I asked the middle-aged Norwegian groom if he had everything he wanted, and he said, in halting heavily accented English, that he was contented. I left him sitting on his hay bale staring mindlessly into space, and went on with my rounds. The horses were all travelling quietly, munching peacefully at their haynets, oblivious to rocketing round the world at 600 mph. There is no sensation of speed if you can't see an environment rushing past.

We arrived without incident at Kennedy airport, where a gum-chewing customs man came on board with three helpers. He spoke slowly, every second word an 'uh', but he was sharply thorough with the horses. All their papers were in order however, and we began the unloading without more ado. There was the extra job of leading all the horses through a tray of disinfectant before they could set foot on American soil, and while I was seeing to it I heard the customs man asking the Norwegian groom about a work permit, and the halting reply that he was staying for a fortnight only, for a holiday, the kindness of the man who owned the horse.

It was the first time I too had been to the States, and I envied him his fortnight.. Owing to the five hours time difference, it was only six in the evening, local time, when we landed at Kennedy, and we were due to leave again at six next morning; which gave me about nine free hours in which to see New York. Although to my body mechanism it was already bedtime, I didn't waste any of them in sleeping.

The only snag to this was having to start another full day's work with eyes requiring matchsticks. Billy yawned over making the boxes as much as I did and only the third member of the team, the deaf elderly Alf, had had any rest. Since even if one shouted he could hear very little, the three of us worked in complete silence like robots, isolated in our own thoughts, with gaps as unbridgeable between us as between like poles of magnets. Unlike poles attract, like poles repel. Billy and I were a couple of cold Norths.

There was a full load going back again, as was usual on Yardman trips from one continent to another. He hated wasting space, and was accustomed to telephone around the studs when a long flight was on the books, to find out if they had anything to send or collect. The customers all liked it, for on full long distance loads Yardman made a reduction in the fares. Timmie and Conker had less cheerful views of this practice, and I now saw why. One's body didn't approve of tricks with the clock. But at the point of no return way out over the Atlantic I shed my drowsiness in one leaping heartbeat, and with horror had my first introduction to a horse going berserk in mid-air.

Old Alf shook my shoulder, and the fright in his face brought me instantly to my feet. I went where he pointed, up towards the nose of the aircraft.

In the second to front box a solidly-muscled 3-year-old colt had pulled his head collar to pieces and was standing free and untied in the small wooden square. He had his head down, his forelegs straddled, and he was kicking out with his hind feet in a fixed, fearful rhythm. White foamy sweat stood out all over him and he was squealing. The companion beside him was trying in a terrified way to escape, his eyes rolling and his body pushing hard against the wooden side of the box.

The colt's hooves thudded against the back wall of the box like battering rams. The wooden panels shook and rattled and began to splinter. The metal bars banding the sides together strained at the corner lynch pins, and it only needed one to break for the whole thing to start disintegrating.

I found the co-pilot at my elbow, yelling urgently.

'Captain says how do you expect him to fly the aircraft with all this thumping going on. He says to keep that horse still, it's affecting the balance.'

'How?' I asked.

'That's your affair,' he pointed out. 'And for God's sake do something about it quickly.'

The back wall of the colt's box cracked from top to bottom. The pieces were still held in place by the guy chains, but at the present rate they wouldn't hold more than another minute, and then we should have on our minds a maddened animal loose in a pressurised aircraft with certain death to us all if he got a hoof through a window.

'Have you got a humane killer on board?' I said.

'No. This is usually a passenger craft. Why don't you bring your own?'

There were no rules to say one had to take a humane killer in animal transport. There should be. But it was too late to regret it.

'We've got drugs in the first aid kit,' the co-pilot suggested.

I shook my head. 'They're unpredictable. Just as likely to make him worse.' It might even have been a tranquilliser which started him off, I thought fleetingly. They often backfired with horses. And it would be quite impossible in any case to inject even a safe drug through a fine needle designed for humans into a horse as wild as this.

'Get a carving knife or something from the galley,' I said. 'Anything long and sharp. And quick.'

He turned away, stumbling in his haste. The colt's hind feet smashed one broken half of the wall clean out. He turned round balefully, thrust his head between the top and centre banding bars, and tried to scramble through. The panic in his eyes was pitiful.

From inside his jerkin Billy calmly produced a large pistol and pointed it towards the colt's threshing head.

'Don't be a bloody fool,' I shouted. 'We're 30,000 ft up.'

The co-pilot came back with a white handled saw-edged bread knife, saw the gun, and nearly fainted.

'D . . . don't,' he stuttered. 'D . . . d . . . don't.'

Billy's eyes were very wide. He was looking fixedly at the heaving colt and hardly seemed to hear. All his mind seemed to be concentrated on aiming the gun that could kill us all.

The colt smashed the first of the lynch pins and lunged forwards, bursting out of the remains of the box like flood water from a dam. I snatched the knife from the co-pilot and as the horse surged towards me stuck the blade into the only place available, the angle where the head joined the neck.

I hit by some miracle the carotid artery. But I couldn't get out of his way afterwards. The colt came down solidly on top of me, pouring blood, flailing his legs and rolling desperately in his attempts to stand up again.

His mane fell in my mouth and across my eyes, and his heaving weight crushed the breath in and out of my lungs like some nightmare form of artificial respiration. He couldn't right himself over my body, and as his struggles weakened he eventually got himself firmly wedged between the remains of his own box and the one directly aft of it. The co-pilot bent down and put his hands under my arm-pits and in jerks dragged me out from underneath.

The blood went on pouring out, hot sticky gallons of it, spreading down the gangways in scarlet streams. Alf cut open one of the hay bales and began covering it up, and it soaked the hay into a sodden crimson brown mess. I don't know how many pints of blood there should be in a horse: the colt bled to death and his heart pumped out nearly every drop.

My clothes were soaked in it, and the sweet smell made me feel sick. I stumbled down the plane into the lavatory compartment and stripped to the skin, and washed myself with hands I found to be helplessly trembling. The door opened without ceremony, and the co-pilot thrust a pair of trousers into my arms. His overnight civvies.

'Here,' he said. 'Compliments of the house.'

I nodded my thanks, put them on, and went back up the plane, soothing the restive frightened horses on the way.

The co-pilot was arguing with Billy about whether Billy would really have pulled the trigger, and Billy was saying a bullet from a revolver wouldn't make a hole in a metal aircraft. The co-pilot cursed, said you couldn't risk it, and mentioned ricochets and glass windows. But what I wanted to know, though I didn't ask, was what was Billy doing carrying a loaded pistol round with him in an underarm holster as casually as a wallet.

Chapter Eight

A Ride at Sandown

John Hislop

After the tragedy of Mississippi my career as an amateur rider stood still. I had one or two rides – pretty indifferent ones – in point-to-points, but no winners, and no one seemed to want my services under N.H. Rules.

But one day Tom Masson rang me up with thrilling news: 'I've got you a ride in an amateurs' chase at Sandown, for Jack Reardon, on Tremolite.'

Tremolite was a horse whom Tom had summered for Jack Reardon and was a useful 'chaser in his class. If all went well he seemed certain to win.

A week before the race I went down to Epsom to ride the horse at school. I stayed the night with Jack Reardon and was enchanted with his perfectly-kept little house and yard, as neat and spruce as himself; so quiet and secluded, yet only just outside Epsom.

Every training centre has its particular characteristics and Epsom is as different from Newmarket as is

Maisons-Laffitte from Chantilly. After the starched and disciplined atmosphere of the Heath, the Downs had a carefree air, in keeping with the gipsies which throng them during Derby week.

No one, whether lads or trainers, seemed to mind particularly what they wore; and the horses were not, as a whole, so well turned out or of so high a quality as at Newmarket, though none, at any centre, ever looked better than those trained by Jack Reardon.

I had never ridden out at a training stable away from Newmarket, and the experience thrilled me. It was a beautiful morning early in October, and something of the colour and warmth of summer still lingered as we rode up towards the schooling fences, Jack Reardon telling me about the horse and how he went best.

'He must be covered up till as late as possible. If he sees daylight he's gone, he's so keen to get on with the job. And if you show him a fence too far away he's so anxious to get to it he forgets about jumping it properly. But if you keep a good, steady hold of him, tuck him in behind and only show him the fence the last few strides he's a great ride.'

I still had a phobia about not being able to hold horses who pulled hard. It was less acute than formerly, but always present in my mind; and Jack Reardon's word nudged it back into prominence. As I looked at Tremolite's powerful, muscular neck and sensed the resolution in his bold head and strong devouring stride, I began to feel a little doubtful.

However, I survived a couple of canters and jumping three or four schooling fences without mishap, though the pace of the school was directed by Tremolite and not by me, being considerably faster than was intended.

I thought that I sensed a suspicion of doubt in Jack's question: 'Well, how did you like him?' after I pulled up. But I did not want to show any sign of ebbing confidence, in case someone else should be given the ride on the day. So I said as gaily and carelessly as possible: 'Fine, he's a grand ride!'

Once more, the days of anticipation began. How much of a jockey's life is anticipation! And for me, who always found it weighing so heavily on my mind, it seemed, at times, intolerable. First, waiting to know whether you have got the ride. Then, the passing of the days, the hours and, finally, the minutes, before being called out. With three or four rides a day it was better, but nerves never left me alone completely, and there have been times when I have sat in the jockey's room before a race, the muscles of my legs trembling and twitching as if with ague, the sweat soaking my armpits and the thought: 'God, why do I do this?' going round in my head like a frantic, caged squirrel.

I do not think it was fear alone; because, strangely enough, as my nerve began to fail my pre-race anxiety became no worse, but it was always there, and only vanished completely when the gate went up and the race was on.

Geoff knew of my impending ride and, on the day, as we sat down to breakfast with the morning papers after going out with the first lot, he said:

'Hear what comfortable words *The Times* saith,' opening that paper at the racing page and, by no tremor of expression showing that he was making up the words, announcing:

'Tremolite is a difficult horse to ride and no mount for an amateur; I cannot be hopeful of his chances.'

He betrayed himself by bursting out laughing as soon as he had finished, but his remark was more prophetic than he realised. Still, there were several hours to go before its possible fulfilment and I determined to put away, as far as possible, any thought of impending disaster. The immediate outlook was certainly a pleasing one. Ted Leader, then an eminent professional, who had won the Grand National on Sprig, had promised to give me a lift to Sandown, and, to make the prospect more enjoyable, he was going to pick up a beautiful and charming actress, Ann Todd, in London, and take her to Sandown as well.

With an excellent chance of winning – based on Tremolite's ability, not my jockeyship – it seemed that perhaps this was really going to be my day.

The early stages went delightfully. From London to Newmarket, Ted Leader listened patiently to my conversation, which was chiefly about my riding history and aspirations, and talked to me as if I was a rider of equal skill and experience.

Miss Todd proved as beautiful and gracious off the stage as on it and, when we stopped for a drink at the Ace of Spades on the Kingston-by-pass, I felt a sense of distinction at the heads turned towards us, in recognition of two such well-known figures in the world of the stage and the Turf.

At Sandown Jack Reardon handed me over to Gerry Hardy, a really good jockey who was then riding for the stable. A year or two later he had a terrible fall at Plumpton, which ended his career.

'This is John Hislop; he's riding Tremolite in the last. Take him to Charlie and ask him to fix him up.'

'Feeling strong? This horse takes a bit of riding when

he's well – and, I can tell you, he's well today,' Gerry Hardy remarked as we walked across to the weighing room. The observation did not increase my confidence.

'Here you are, Charlie, another client for you – if he survives – he's riding Tremolite for Jack Reardon in the last,' Gerry Hardy said as he led me up to the valet. 'This is Charlie Stalker; he'll see to you. Charlie, this is Mr Hislop.'

Thus began an association and friendship which lasted until Charlie Stalker died a year or two before I gave up riding. To any jockey, but especially to one who rides over fences and hurdles, his valet is one of the most important people in his life. The valet looks after all his riding tack – saddles, boots, breeches, skull cap, whip, underclothes and so on – keeps it in repair and clean, and ensures that it gets to whichever meetings the jockey is riding at.

It was once said that the three most efficient organisations in the world were the German Army, the British Navy and the Roman Catholic Church; to these should be added the racecourse valeting system. Though having experienced its benefits over twenty years, I have never quite grasped the miracle of its achievements: how breeches, boots and saddles which were soaking wet and plastered with mud at 4 o'clock on Wednesday at Plumpton, are produced clean and dry by noon at Nottingham on Thursday. The secret is hard, fast work, wonderful co-ordination and the accepted agreement among jockeys to pool their spare tack. If your own tack is not ready or available, say, because a ride materialises at the last moment at a meeting which you had not planned to attend, the valet looking after you will always produce the necessary equipment from somewhere. Every southern valet has his opposite number in the north, and a jockey's tack passes from one to another by what seems a magic process. Not only is the efficiency and comfort of a jockey's riding life dependent upon his valet, but his safety too. A broken girth could cost a jockey his life, let alone a race.

Apart from the mechanical and business side of the arrangement, the personality and character of a valet is an important and influential factor in a jockey's career. In a profession in which, often, nerves are on edge, tempers are frayed and pain and despondency alternate with exhilaration and success, tact and understanding on the part of a valet can be worth much.

All this I was to discover later.

'Right, Sir; I'll put you over here,' Charlie said to me, leading me over to his pitch. It was the one in the far left-hand corner of the room facing you as you walk through from the scale, near the fireplace.

'Give us your things. You haven't got a saddle, have you? Well, I'll fix you up.'

Charlie was a white-haired elderly man with a reddish face and bald on top, giving him a slightly monastic look. He was probably younger than he appeared for he never seemed to change all the time he looked after me – but he must have been getting on in years, for he used to 'do' the great Tich Mason, who won the National on Kirkland in 1905. He had a good clientele: Peter Boswick, the American owner-rider – one of the best amateurs I have seen, though he nearly always rode good horses – Danny Morgan, Evan Williams, Eric Brown, Hector Gordon, Staff Ingham, Gerry Hardy, Bruce Hobbs, were some of the riders he valeted in that era.

Whether amateurs or professionals, Charlie treated all his jockeys alike, except that he would sometimes address the amateurs as 'Sir', 'Guvnor' or 'Mister' during his less busy moments. While there were valets who were more attentive to the less important, material needs of their clients, such as helping jockeys to dress, no one had a deeper personal interest in his patrons than Charlie, or took more trouble when he was really needed.

If you had a bad fall and were taken to the ambulance room, he always came round at once to see how you were and whether he could do anything for you. Emerging from mists of unconsciousness, or while the doctor was trying to discover whether you had any broken bones or not, it was always a comfort to see Charlie's familiar, anxious face in the background.

'Don't worry, Guv: I'll get someone to drive your car home if you're not too good; and if you've got to go to hospital I'll ring home and tell them not to get anxious. I'll be in to see you tomorrow evening.'

Never downhearted himself, he always seemed to make the outlook less bleak when you ran into a bad patch: when good jumpers fell with you, apparent certainties got beaten and other jockeys were put up in your place.

'Never mind, your luck'll change.'

He knew the moods and ways of all his jockeys, was deeply loyal to them and made allowances for the irritability and bad temper which the exigencies of the game aroused in us all sometimes.

Jockeys seldom change their valets, and the latter and their clients form separate, individualistic coteries, rather in the manner of houses at a public school. If you did not have a ride yourself, or had no other personal interest, you instinctively hoped that one of Charlie's jockeys would win. If you were asked to recommend another rider, you would suggest one of Charlie's jockeys for choice. And in the same way that there was a tendency at school to look with faint disparagement upon the members of rival factions, there was an inclination to regard the clique sharing one's own valet as superior to others: 'That's a dodgy crowd Arthur does – he got paid with another bouncer last week.'

'That lot of George's seem to think they own the racecourse, just because there's a Lord among them.'

And as, at school, boys grew up and left, others rising in seniority, the older jockeys would retire and the younger ones move to the more favoured places – the one in the corner that Staff Ingham always had, or the one near the fire, instead of bordering on the next pitch, where the valet would shove the 'chalk jockeys' and bumpers who rode about once a year. The latter were sometimes soldiers and brought a batman, who got in everyone's way and was liable to tread on your bare feet with ammunition boots.

On this day I was the most junior of the riders looked after by Charlie, and felt it. Though I had been in racing two or three years and knew a good many flat-racing trainers and jockeys, the jumping world was largely unknown to me, and I a stranger to it. I was treated as were – perhaps they still are – young officers on joining certain regiments; that is to say, ignored.

Having left my tack with Charlie, I went off to see the preceding races. Mine was the last and I wished it had been the first, as I could not concentrate upon or enjoy the racing thinking about it.

The first race was won by a horse trained by Jack Reardon called Gloria Mia, who was ridden by Gerry Hardy. It seemed a good omen.

The afternoon dragged its way through one race after another. I went to get ready before the fifth – jockeys usually change before the race preceding the one in which they are first riding; this gives time both to watch the previous race and to weigh out without rushing.

Charlie kept an eye on me while I dressed, to see that I indulged in no eccentricity which would reflect on him. If not watched, the uninitiated, whether amateur or professional, are liable to strange unpredictable sartorial habits: supporting their breeches with belts or braces, dispensing with 'elastics' (elastic bands worn round the wrists to keep the sleeves of the jacket from flapping about) or wearing a coloured scarf. The colours provided for me were in the form of a roll-neck sweater, the most common for N.H. racing, and I was proposing not to wear the customary white scarf round my neck as it seemed to serve no purpose.

'You put it on,' Charlie said firmly. 'It helps to keep you warm and might save you a broken neck.' And giving me no chance to argue he took the one he had provided for me and tied it round my neck.

The rest of the day's proceedings followed the pattern to which I was becoming resigned.

'I've put a chain-snaffle on him. It'll give you a better chance of steadying him,' Jack Reardon remarked to me in the parade-ring. The words had an uncomfortable portent, which was soon realised: Tremolite ran away with me on the way to the post.

The true nature of the circumstance might not have been obvious to the casual observer, because I did not wish to reveal the truth by sitting up and sawing at his mouth, but I knew only too well that the horse was in absolute charge. Those familiar with the topography of Sandown Park will remember there is a high, boarded fence behind the start of the two-mile 'chase course. This was my salvation. I aimed Tremolite at it, and since it was unjumpable and the other runners were pulling up, he came to a halt. The crisis was over, but the signs for the immediate future were not good.

I considered pulling up my leathers to give me a better purchase for holding Tremolite, but thought by so doing I would increase the chance of my falling off if he hit a fence, so left them as they were.

In order to give myself some hope of carrying out my orders to wait, I lined up behind the others – it is no bad plan on a hard-pulling horse who has to be covered up. Somehow, probably because I jammed him behind a wall of horses and he had no option but to stay there, I succeeded in keeping Tremolite behind the leaders over the first two fences, which he barely saw and jumped as if they were hurdles. As we swung away from the stands and ran down the hill to the first fence of the three miles, Tremolite gathered momentum. My skull cap flew off in the rush of wind against us, for by that time I was sitting up like a Life Guardsman, sawing at his mouth in a desperate but hopeless attempt to steady him. He barged his way past the horse in front of him, thereby getting a clear view of the fence ahead. The sight was too rich for his blood. Lengthening his stride and taking an even stronger hold of his bit he went at it like a determined rugby football player going for the try-line. This was the last I remembered.

I became vaguely aware of the ambulance swaying

and bumping its way back. Then I must have become unconscious again; for I only remember coming round in the ambulance room. 'He's all right except for a bit of concussion,' the course doctor said to Charlie when the latter came in a few minutes later. And to me: 'Go to bed when you get home, and ask your doctor to see you tomorrow. You'd better take it easy for a few days.'

'Here's a cup of tea; you'll feel better when you've drunk it.' And Charlie handed me the cup, having shepherded me back to the dressing-room, where I was putting on my clothes in a dazed way. 'We've got you a lift back to Newmarket, but do as he said: go easy, and see the doctor tomorrow. You've had a fair knock and concussion isn't a thing you want to monkey about with.'

When I found, on the way back, that for a short period I could not speak properly, as do people who have had a stroke, I realised that there was something in the theory. And when the doctor saw me at Newmarket he made me go to bed for a week. Otherwise, except for a chipped tooth, which Doctor Cootes patched up, discoursing meanwhile upon the dangers with which steeplechasing and hunting were fraught, no material damage was done. But the future of my riding career seemed bleaker than ever. I noted, with mortification, that when next Jack Reardon ran a horse in a 'bumpers' race he put up Roger Corbett, a contemporary of mine at Wellington, where he was chiefly known as a rugby football forward – not surprisingly, he had great difficulty with his weight during his riding career. He was a first-rate amateur, but was killed in a motor accident. The horse won, which made it worse for me.

Chapter Nine

The Zebras

Roy Campbell

From the dark woods that breathe of fallen showers,
Harnessed with level rays in golden reins,
The zebras draw the dawn across the plains
Wading knee-deep among the scarlet flowers.
The sunlight, zithering their flanks with fire,
Flashes between the shadows as they pass
Barred with electric tremors through the grass
Like wind along the golden strings of a lyre.

Into the flushed air snorting rosy plumes
That smoulder round their feet in drifting fumes,
With dove-like voices call the distant fillies,
While round the herds the stallion wheels his flight,
Engine of beauty volted with delight,
To roll his mare among the trampled lilies.

Chapter Ten

The Old Firm

R. C. Lyle

Brown Jack began the season of 1933 as if he was a youngster in the prime of life. To those who ask what is the secret of his perennial youth, I can only point to his breeding, his courage, his perfect soundness, his remarkable intelligence, and the kindliness and sweetness of his temperament. At the age of nine he looked, and was the embodiment of youth. Like every one of us he was racing with age, and his courage and soundness put him well in the handicap: with ears pricked and dancing his little two-step of delight he had got age beaten. And though it is not recorded in the Annals of the Turf, I will wager that the Judge gave him the verdict by many lengths. And in this long race Steve Donoghue, I know, is associated with him: it is his victory too.

I have referred on more than one occasion to Brown Jack's soundness. Perhaps I ought to add a footnote. He had, as we have seen in an earlier chapter, one slight weakness, and that was not, like Achilles's, in the heel, but in the soles of his feet. The thinness of the soles of his feet in his early days made him very careful on firm going, but in time they grew harder and thicker and troubled him less. Yet he always was careful. He knew that though hard going might not bruise his feet, if he let himself go on it the consequent jarring would make itself felt later, and he was likely to wake up next morning with stiffness and pain in his legs. And that brings me again to his intelligence. He knows exactly whether the ground will suit him or not. If he believes it's too hard, his mind is made up at once: he won't try. Donoghue will tell you that.

It is this intelligent care that he has taken of himself that has enabled him to remain young so long, in spite of leading such a strenuous life.

He began the season once more with a trial trip, on this occasion at Sandown Park on 21st April in the Twickenham Handicap Stakes, a mile and a quarter race. He was not last, but he was nowhere near the leaders.

His next race was for the Rosebery Memorial Plate at Epsom on 30th May. Ivor Anthony was pleased with his condition: he was well forward, and his chance of winning the race that Lord Nugent had wrested from him the previous year was considered by the stable to be good. In 1932 he had had to carry the impossible weight of 10 st. 2 lb., but he had run a magnificent race and was beaten rather by the weight than by Lord Nugent. Lord Nugent, let in so lightly on that occasion, has not, so far as I know, won a race since. Brown Jack this year had been given the rather more reasonable weight of 9 st. 11 lb. Moreover, the course was, Anthony thought, suited to him.

A week before the race Anthony took Brown Jack and Mail Fist down to Salisbury to tune up Brown Jack on a neighbouring gallop. Gordon Richards had the ride on Brown Jack. But Brown Jack was in no mood to exert himself: either he did not like the going or perhaps that particular gallop was familiar to him and he was bored with it: or perhaps he felt that after raising his hopes of excitement by driving him away from Wroughton in the motor horse-box it was letting him down rather badly to bring him to that quiet gallop with only old Mail Fist. Anyhow, he showed very plainly that he had no mind to stir himself, and he gave Gordon Richards a very hard time of it.

'You don't want to have a night out before riding this old fellow,' Richards commented when the work was over. And Ivor Anthony, a man of few words, smiled and nodded, and was in no way discouraged.

How different the story of the race! Gordon Richards was then riding the King's horse Foxearth, a nice four-year-old who was much fancied to win. Donoghue was, of course, on Brown Jack who was set to concede 2 st. to Foxearth, 25 lb. to the five-year-old Roi de Paris, and 30 lb. or more to the other eight runners. Mandritsara, 7 st. 9 lb., started favourite at 85 to 40 against, Foxearth second favourite at 3 to 1 against, while 9 to 1 was offered against Brown Jack's chance.

Here was no dull training gallop, but the excitement of the racecourse, and going much to his liking! Brown Jack was always well placed and going easily. Coming into the Straight Roi de Paris looked all over a winner; but Gordon Richards on the King's horse came up with him, mastered him and went to the front. Then 'the old firm' began their challenge – halfway down the

Straight they came with a great run in the middle of the course. Richards on Foxearth rode hard, but his mount was 'left standing' by the youthful veteran who was conceding him 28 lb. Long before the winning post was reached Brown Jack had won the race, and he passed the post with ears pricked as usual, amidst great cheering. He was easing up before the end, knowing full well that he had won. When he and Donoghue came back to the unsaddling enclosure there was again much clapping of hands. Brown Jack looked around taking it all in in the nicely proud manner of one who is accustomed to applause but none the less appreciates it.

Later His Majesty the King sent for Brown Jack's owner and, in congratulating him, said, 'Although everybody likes winning races, nobody could possibly object to being beaten by such a great horse as Brown Jack.'

Well done, indeed, Brown Jack! It should be added that Gordon Richards, in spite of that training gallop a week before the race, was not at all surprised that Brown Jack had beaten him. He knew 'the old firm' was still a force to be reckoned with.

Brown Jack's performance at Epsom seems to have scared away his possible Ascot opponents. The Ascot meeting followed a fortnight after Epsom, and from the moment he won at Epsom his success in the Queen Alexandra Stakes for the fifth year in succession was generally accepted as a racing certainty. For the first time there appeared to be no serious challenge to this his prescriptive right. Mail Fist was there, of course, but there were only two other runners besides Brown Jack – Corn Belt and Sigiri.

It was a great and memorable afternoon. To everyone's delight the King won a race with Limelight early in the afternoon. And then, in the last race but one of the afternoon, and of the meeting, Brown Jack made his sixth successful appearance at Ascot. It was not a race to bet on – it was a race to watch with admiration and respect. In the paddock beforehand all eyes were fixed on the youthful old gentleman. He was as well groomed as any gentleman at the meeting. To say that he was well preserved would be untrue: it suggests a conscious and careful if successful battle with age; whereas Brown Jack looked as young and fit and handsome and carefree as any three-year-old. We watched him and wondered whether we were not back in 1928 when he had been led round the paddock before winning the Ascot Stakes. He was as good to look upon now as then, and now as then he showed his awareness of the greatness of the occasion by shaking at the knees and sweating while he was being saddled. He still had that youthful desire to get on with the job which had distinguished him as a four-year-old.

Donoghue tells me that he has known but one other horse behave as he does when he mounts him. 'He puts on inches,' he says. 'He is relaxed when I come to him, but as I mount him you can see his veins swell. He grows in stature, rises to meet me.' And Donoghue adds with typical exaggeration, 'He is like that before I mount him' – holding his hand about 3 ft from the ground – 'but when I'm on his back he's well over sixteen hands. In all my experience of riding, only that great filly Diadem gave me a similar impression.'

And so the familiar pair, Brown Jack and Mail Fist, both technically described on the race card as 'aged', canter down to the starting gate with the 5-year-old Corn Belt and the 4-year-old Sigiri, and the good wishes of everyone present. Brown Jack, it may be mentioned, started at the impossible odds of 5 to 1 on, but, as I have already said, the betting on such an event is of no importance.

As for so many years, Mail Fist took the lead at the start and made the pace for Brown Jack for the first two miles. Then, at the same spot as ever – in the Swinley Bottom – he retired gracefully from the scene with his job well done, and Brown Jack took the lead. Presently, to everyone's amazement, Sigiri had the temerity, almost it must be recorded, the impertinence, to go after him. Corn Belt, with more respect, followed quietly behind. Brown Jack came into the Straight with his ears pricked still closely attended by Sigiri. Not only did Sigiri hang on well, but soon afterwards, if you please, he dared to challenge Brown Jack. In a moment Brown Jack shook him off; and Sigiri, properly shattered, retired from the contest. All up the Straight Brown Jack galloped with evident enjoyment, knowing that the cheering and the clapping of hands were for him. I think that on this occasion he may suddenly have become a little swollen-headed, for he began to take matters very easily a long way from the winning post. It was an old habit of his to ease up the moment he thought he had won the race. But never before surely had he eased up so early. He was treating the race as if it were a walk-over! The effrontery of it made us smile even while we clapped our hands and cheered.

But Brown Jack had miscalculated this time. J. Childs on Corn Belt, who had been going along quietly behind, quickly sized up the situation: he realised that there was a chance of Brown Jack stopping almost to a walk, and at the Distance he brought Corn Belt with one of his typical runs. The gap between the two horses shortened and shortened. Corn Belt got almost to Brown Jack's quarters. The cheering and the clapping of hands ceased abruptly: the anxiety of the great crowd grew big in that moment of silence. It appeared that Ascot might end in tragedy.

But Brown Jack had his great rider and friend, Donoghue, on his back. Donoghue knew his gallant friend's idiosyncrasies. He was at once alive to the looming danger. Brown Jack must be brought down to earth. Donoghue showed him his whip. Brown Jack at once realised that there must be something terribly wrong. He gathered himself together, pricked his ears, did that curious little two-step shuffle and, accompanied by a renewed outburst of cheering, went away from the outrageous intruder who had dared to interfere with his royal progress to the winning post!

Of the reception given to Brown Jack and Donoghue there is nothing new to be recorded. They were received back to the unsaddling enclosure with hats raised and much cheering and clapping of hands. Sir Harold Wernher and his wife received the pair. Ivor Anthony, as bashful and as modest as ever, waited until everything was almost over before he came into the unsaddling enclosure to take just one look at his charge. Then, when everything was found to be in order, Brown Jack turned and walked out of the unsaddling enclosure knowing full well that, so far as he was concerned, another Ascot was over. There was more quiet cheering and clapping of hands as he went out.

Brown Jack had done what no horse had ever done before: he had won at Ascot in six successive years: and in five successive years he had won the Queen Alexandra

Stakes. And on each occasion Donoghue had shared the victory with him. I make no excuse for repeating these statements, nor for emphasising again the remarkable nature of the achievement. There was still no horse in training whose stamina and courage were equal to the youthful 9-year-old's.

That a much larger public than that that attends the race meetings was following his career is testified to by his daily mail, which comes from all parts of the Empire and the world. Brown Jack's mail is as large as that of a popular film star. Bad poems and good wishes are showered upon him. He has been asked to grace charity bazaars with his presence and, I believe, to lend the lustre of his name to patent foods and medicines. And his letters are a revelation of the fortunes great and small that he has made for faithful punters. He has provided thousands of unexpected holidays; and extravagances and necessities of every kind, from a shoot in Scotland to a badly needed new armchair in the kitchen, have been his gifts. But it is not only as a financial benefactor that he is appreciated. His mail shows that the qualities that have characterised his racing career are generally recognised. Here is just one letter, typical of hundreds, that reveals this:

Dear Sir Harold Wernher,

Thank you so much for your kindness in replying to my request for a photo of Brown Jack. I love the likeness and intend to have it framed and hung over my piano (1) for luck, (2) to inspire my pupils with ambition and pluck! to fight on to the end.

Chapter Eleven

The Invasion

Leo Tolstoy

The first white frosts had laid their thin film of ice over the earth which was soaked with autumn rains. Where the grass had been trodden, or grew thickly, it stood out in patches of bright green, in the fields where the cattle had been feeding, and the withered haulms of the summer's wheat streaked the pale tints of the spring crops chequered by russet plots of buck-wheat. The woods, still densely clothed with verdure till the end of August, like islands surrounded by stubbly fields and black earth ploughed for sowing, were now crimson and gold, and showed in vivid contrast against the tender green of sprouting corn. The hare was changing his fur, young foxes were quitting the nest, and the wolf cubs were by this time as big as large dogs. It was the height of the hunting season.

Our young Nimrod's pack of hounds, though well trained, had already been rather hard worked, so by common consent it was agreed that they should have three days' rest and that on the 16th September they would have a day out, beginning at Doubrava, where they were certain to find a litter of wolf-cubs.

In the course of the 14th the cold rapidly increased, and during the day there was a sharp frost, but towards evening the air grew softer and a thaw set in, so that on the morning of the 15th, when Nicholas, wrapped in his dressing-gown, looked out at a very early hour, the weather was all he could wish, perfect hunting weather: the grey sky seemed to melt, to flow, to be softly falling; there was not a breath of air; the beads of dropping mist, so fine as to be almost invisible, rested for an instant on the leafless twigs with a transient sparkle and then trickled down till they were caught on the leaves that slowly fluttered off one by one. The garden soil was as black and shining as jet in the foreground, and at a short distance disappeared under the grey, damp shroud of mist. Nicholas stepped on to the balcony, where everything was dripping with moisture; on the air came the smell of the kennel, and the peculiar fragrance of forests in autumn where everything is fading and dying. Milka, the great black-and-tan bitch, with heavy hind-quarters and large prominent eyes, got up when she saw her master, stretched herself and crouched; then, with one leap she bounded up and licked his face, while another borzoi, with his stern in the air, came galloping up from the garden at a top pace to run against Nicholas.

At the same moment a loud 'Ohoi!' rang through the air – the peculiar halloo of the hunter, a mixture of bass notes and a shrill crow, and round the corner of the house came Danilo the huntsman, a man of wrinkled aspect, with hair cropped close after the fashion of Little Russia. He carried a long whip; his expression was that of thorough contempt for things in general – a look rarely seen in any but huntsmen. He took off his cap in his master's presence, but his expression did not alter – indeed, it had no trace of insolence. Nicholas knew very well that this stalwart fellow with his scornful mien was his man, a hunter after his own heart!

'Hey there, Danilo!' he shouted, at once carried away by the irresistible passion for the chase, the day made on purpose, the sight of the dogs and the huntsman, and forgetting all his good resolutions as a lover forgets everything in his mistress's presence.

'What are your orders, excellency?' replied a deep bass voice, hoarse with shouting to the dogs, and two bright black eyes were fixed on the face of the young count who remained silent: 'Will he resist the temptation?' those eyes seemed to say.

'Well – a good day for a hunt?' said Nicholas, pulling Milka's ears.

'Ouvarka was out at daybreak,' said the bass voice, after a moment's pause. 'He says she went off into the plantation at Otradnoe. He heard them howling.'

This meant that a she-wolf he had tracked had gone into the wood with her cubs; the plantation was detached from the rest of the property, and lay about two versts off.

'We must go after her. What do you think! Bring up Ouvarka.'

'Very good.'

'Stop – give them nothing to eat.'

'All right.'

Five minutes later Danilo and Ouvarka came into

the sitting room. Danilo was not remarkably tall, and yet, strange to say, he looked in a room very much as a horse or a bear might look in the midst of domestic furniture. He himself was conscious of it; he kept as close as possible to the door, spoke as low as he could, tried to keep still for fear of breaking something, and made haste to say all he had to say that he might get into the open air again and under the wide sky, instead of standing under the ceiling which seemed to crush him.

Nicholas having questioned the men, and being told again and again that the pack would be better for a run – Danilo himself was dying to be off – ordered the horses to be brought round. Just as the huntsman was quitting the room Natacha rushed in. She was not brushed or dressed; she had thrown her old nurse's great shawl round her.

'You are starting! I said so. Sonia said no. I was sure you would be off to take advantage of such a perfect day!'

'Yes,' said Nicholas reluctantly; for he meant work and did not want to take either Petia or Natacha. 'We are going after a wolf – it will not amuse you.'

'On the contrary – you know it will. It is very mean of you to have the horses saddled and never say a word to us.'

'The Russian who ignores all obstacles – hurrah! On we go!' shouted Petia, who had followed his sister.

'But you know mamma will not let you go.'

'I shall go – I will go, whatever she says,' replied Natacha, resolutely. 'Danilo, order out my horse, and tell Mikailo to bring round my leash of hounds.'

Danilo, very uncomfortable at finding himself under a roof, was completely abashed at receiving an order from the young lady; he cast down his eyes and tried to make his escape without seeming to hear, taking great care, however, not to run against her or hit her by some clumsy movement.

The old count, though he had always kept up a hunting establishment on a grand footing, had ceased to hunt since he had placed it in his son's hands; however, on this 15th of September, feeling well and in good spirits, he decided on joining the party.

The hunters and horses were soon assembled in front of the house. Nicholas as he passed Natacha and Petia was too much absorbed in his arrangements to heed what they said to him. How could a man be expected to think of trifles at such a serious moment? He saw to everything himself, sent forward the huntsmen with the hounds, mounted his chestnut horse Donetz, and whistling to his own dogs, rode off across country towards the plantation. A groom followed leading a dark bay mare which the old count was to ride, after driving to a certain rendezvous in his drosky.

Fifty-four hounds with forty greyhounds and several dogs in leash, six huntsmen and a whole troop of keepers – in all 130 dogs and twenty horsemen, set forth at once. Each dog knew whom he was to obey, and answered to his name; each man knew what he was to do and where he was to stand. When they had quitted the park they silently turned down the high road, but soon left it for the fields, where the horses' hooves sank noiselessly into the deep turf or splashed up the water in the puddles in the lanes. The dull mist was still falling; the whistle of a huntsman rang now and then through the still air – a horse whinnied, a long whip cracked sharply and the truant dog thus recalled to duty whined plaintively. The cavalcade had gone about half-way when suddenly a party of five or more horsemen emerged from the fog, followed by their dogs, and joined the Rostows; at their head rode a handsome old man of dignified mien, with a long thick grey moustache.

'Good morning, little uncle!' said Nicholas.

'A sure find! . . . Forward, quick march!' said the newcomer, a small proprietor of the neighbourhood and distantly related to the Rostows. 'I was quite certain – I said you would be sure to come out; and you were in the right. It is a sure find . . . Forward, quick march!' he repeated – his favourite watchword. 'Close round the wood as soon as possible, for my man tells me that the Illaguines are out near Korniki and they might carry off the whole litter under your nose. . . . But it is a sure find. Forward, quick march!'

'I am going straight there. Shall we get our packs together?' The order was given, and the two horsemen rode on, side by side.

Natacha, with a shawl wrapped round her so that nothing was to be seen of her eager face but the sparkling eyes, soon came up with them, followed by Petia, Mikailo the huntsman, and a stable lad, who served her as body-guard. Petia laughed without rhyme or reason and teased his pony with his whip. Natacha, graceful and firm in her saddle, checked her steed's ardour with a practised hand; a handsome Arab, with a lustrous coat.

The 'little uncle' cast a disapproving side-glance at the youngsters, for wolf-hunting is a serious business and allows no frivolities.

'Good morning, little uncle; we are of the party you see!' cried Petia.

'Good morning, good morning. Don't ride the dogs down,' said the old man sternly.

'Nicholas, what a dear beast Trounila is! He knew me at once,' said Natacha, whistling to her favourite dog.

'In the first place, Trounila is not a beast but a wolf-hound,' said Nicholas, with a glance which was intended to convey to his sister a due sense of his superiority, and the gulf between him and her. She understood.

'We shall not be in your way, little uncle,' she went on. 'We will get in no one's way; we will stay where we are posted without stirring.'

'Nothing can be wiser, little countess. Only mind you do not fall off your horse, for if you do it will be a sure find – no picking you up again! Forward, quick march!'

By this time they were within 200 yds. of the plantation. Rostow and the little uncle having decided from which side the pack should be started, Nicholas pointed out a place where Natacha might stand – and whence, in all probability, she would see nothing – and pushed on beyond a little ravine.

'Steady, little nephew; the old one is the mother! Do not let her slip!'

'You will see,' replied Rostow. 'Hi, Karae!' he called to a dog, hideous from old age but safe to fly at a she-wolf, even when alone.

The old count knew by experience what an eager hunter his son was, and he made haste to join the party; hardly had each man taken his place when the drosky came rolling easily across the level ground, and set down Count Ilia Andreievitch on the spot he had chosen for himself beforehand. His face was ruddy and his spirits high; he tucked up his fur cloak, and heavily mounted his steady old mare, desiring the coachman to take the carriage home again. He was not a very keen sportsman, but he adhered to all the rules of the hunt; he took up his position on the skirts of the wood, gathered up the reins in his left hand, settled himself in the saddle, and, his arrangements being complete, looked about him with a smile. . . . He was ready.

By his side was his body-servant Semione Tchekmar, a good horseman but heavy with years, holding in leash three long-haired, grey Russian wolf-hounds – peculiar breed – keen dogs, though like their master aged, and lying at his feet. About 100 paces off was the count's groom, Mitka, a bold rider and a reckless sportsman. The count, faithful to an old habit, swallowed a dram of capital hunter's brandy, ate a little slice of meat, and washed it down with half a bottle of his favourite Bordeaux. The liquor and the fresh air gave him a colour, his eyes brightened, and as he sat in his short fur jacket, he looked like a child brought out for a treat.

Tchekmar, a lean, hollow-cheeked fellow, having likewise made himself comfortable, looked at his master – for the last thirty years they had been inseparable companions – and seeing him in such a pleasant temper, proceeded to open a conversation as pleasant as his mood. A third person, also on horseback, an old white-bearded man in a woman's pelisse and wearing a preposterously high cap, now came noiselessly to the spot, and drew up a little way behind the count.

'Well, Nastacia Ivanovna' – Nastacia was the buffoon of the neighbourhood – 'mind what you are about. If you frighten the brute you know what Danilo will have to say to you.' The count spoke in a whisper, and winked at the fellow.

'Oh, I have teeth and nails, too,' replied Nastacia Ivanovna.

'Hush – hush!' whispered the count, then turning to Semione he asked: 'Have you seen Natacha Ilinischna? Where is she?'

'With her brother, near the thicket by Yarow: what a treat for her, and she is quite a young lady, too!'

'But is it not wonderful to see her on horseback, Semione? How she rides! She might be a man!'

'It is really wonderful! She is afraid of nothing, and so firm in the saddle!'

'And where is Nicholas?'

'Out by Liadow . . . Never fear, he knows the best places – and what a rider! Danilo and I wonder to see him sometimes!' said Semione, who was very ready to flatter his master.

'Aye, aye, sits a horse well, doesn't he?'

'Quite a picture! The other day, for instance, in the plain by Zavarzine, when he was riding down the fox on that horse of his. It cost a thousand roubles – but the rider is beyond price! And such a handsome fellow! You would have to look a long time to find a match for him!'

'Aye, aye,' said the count again. 'Yes, indeed. . . .'

And he picked up the skirt of his fur cloak and felt in his pocket for his snuff-box.

'Then the other day,' Semione went on, seeing how much pleasure he was giving his master, 'coming out of church, when Michael Sidorocvitch met him . . .' but Semione broke off short; the rush of the pack in hot pursuit, and the barking of some of the dogs struck his ear through the still air; he put down his head and made a sign to the count to keep silence: 'They have found the scent,' he whispered, 'they are going off towards Liadow.'

The count, still smiling over Semione's last speech, sat gazing into the distance with his snuff-box in his hand, without taking a pinch. Danilo's horn warned them that the wolf had been seen; the packs followed close to the three leading hounds, and all gave tongue in the peculiar note that meant they were on the scent of a wolf. The whips now only shouted encouragement. Above all other voices and cries Danilo's was distinctly heard, passing from the deepest bass to the shrillest yell, and loud enough by itself to ring through the wood and far across the country with its cheering call.

The count and his squire soon perceived that the pack had been divided; one half, barking vociferously, was becoming more distant and the others, driven by Danilo, were breaking through the wood at a few paces from where they were posted; presently the direction of the noise told them that the hunt was moving further afield. Semione sighed and freed one of the hounds that was entangled in the leash; the count, too, sighed, and his attention reverting to his snuff-box, he opened it and took a pinch.

'Back!' cried Semione at this instant to one of the dogs that was struggling to make for the open. The count was startled and let his snuff-box fall. Nastacia dismounted and picked it up.

Suddenly – as will happen occasionally – the hunt was coming their way; all those yelping, baying throats seemed to be close in front of them – upon them!

The count looked to the right and caught sight of

Mitka, who, with his eyes starting out of his head, was signalling to him with his cap to look at something in the opposite direction. 'Look out!' he shouted in a voice that was all the louder for long suppression; and slipping the dogs, he rode up at full gallop.

The count and Semione rushed out of the wood, and, on their left, saw the wolf coming towards them at a swinging trot, easy bounds and no appearance of hurry. The excited dogs tore themselves free, and flung themselves on his track.

The brute paused, turned his heavy head to look at them, with the deliberate awkwardness of a man suffering from angina, then, cocking his tail, went on his way and in two leaps vanished in the thicket. At the same moment, from the opposite skirt of the plantation, out came a dog, then another; then the whole pack, astray and puzzled, crossed the clearing in pursuit of the game, and Danilo's chestnut, covered with foam, came pushing his way between the nut-trees. The rider, bending as low as he could, and bareheaded, his grey hair all on end, his face red and streaming, was shouting till his voice cracked to rally the dogs. But when he saw the count his eyes flashed fire. He threatened him with his whip, roaring out a thundering oath: 'Devil take such hunters . . .! To have let the game slip . . .!'

Judging, no doubt, that his master, who looked quite scared, was unworthy of further comment, he let the blow that had been meant for the count fall on the quivering and steaming flank of his innocent steed, and disappeared among the trees after the hounds.

Chapter Twelve

The Donkey

G. K. Chesterton

When fishes flew and forests walked
And figs grew upon thorn,
Some moment when the moon was blood
Then surely I was born.

With monstrous head and sickening cry
And ears like errant wings,
The devil's walking parody
Of all four-footed things.

The tattered outlaw of the earth,
Of ancient crooked will;
Starve, scourge, deride me: I am dumb,
I keep my secret still.

Fools! For I also had my hour;
One far fierce hour and sweet;
There was a shout about my ears,
And palms before my feet.

Chapter Thirteen

Point-to-Point

Dorian Williams

To run a horse in a Point-to-Point you have first to be satisfied that he has not run under National Hunt rules since the preceding 31st December, and secondly you have to register the horse with Messrs Weatherby, who act for the National Hunt Stewards, producing a certificate signed by a Master of Hounds to the effect that the horse has been properly hunted. Most Masters insist that a horse should have been hunted at least eight times. In fact Pancho had been out more than sufficient; anyway the Master, not knowing all our problems, said it was a pleasure to give a certificate to a horse that jumped as Pancho had on the Dewtown Crossroads day, and he wished us luck.

The Point-to-Point was in the last week of March. I decided to start Pancho's training straight away. My plan was for the first month to give him increasingly long, steady road work, with as much trotting uphill as was possible; and this was easy round us as there are plenty of hills. The second month I would start the faster work with a canter twice a week – I knew that the Hickson brothers about eight miles away, who do a great deal of point-to-pointing, would let me use their gallop – gradually working up faster and faster until I was doing a mile and a half at top speed.

All the time the road work would be continued, and then there would be just two weeks for a final tuning up before the first Point-to-Point, which was our own Hunt's and which offered a very handsome cup for the winner of the Members' Race, the Lady Gordon Trophy. This should not really be too difficult to win, always assuming, firstly, that I could get him sufficiently settled down for his road work to be effective; secondly, that I could control him on the gallops; and, thirdly, that I could manage him in a race.

I always rode out to exercise by myself of course, and being alone he gave me practically no trouble. In fact those long solitary rides were as enjoyable as anything I remember. Pancho, I think, loved them too, for he would step briskly out of the yard, his ears pricked, his head up, as if he could not wait to get on with it.

It was early spring, and each day nature seemed to take a step forward. There were the tiny aconites in the hedgerows; then there were the little clusters of snowdrops at the edges of the woods and copses; shy violets on the banks of a lane and, before February was out, the first pale, reluctant primroses. Each day, as one went past certain farms, there were new lambs to be counted; the friskiest and most attractive of all babies, surely – only to grow into the dullest of adults!

Time to contemplate, time to appreciate, time to revel in the March wind skies, the burgeoning of the woodlands, all the aspects of a hibernating countryside gradually coming to life. One day, there were gipsies on the move – Pancho was very suspicious. Another day we ran into hounds, and he was somewhat unsettled for the rest of his work. One brisk morning we saw a cart-mare foal within minutes of its being born; we heard the still air filled with the droning of the saw-mill. There was harrowing, and choirs of white gulls circling, and the caw-caw-cawing of the rooks busy over their nests.

There was Jack the local poacher with his pockets bulging, and his ancient twelve-bore; and the charming sight of Miss Withenshaw driving, as she always did, her little skewbald pony and wicker-work trap. All this was mine to enjoy morning after morning in the delightful, relaxed company of Pancho.

And all the time he was getting fitter and harder. By getting him a late feed just before she went to bed, Sara was now giving him 18 lb of oats, to say nothing of all manner of succulents and stimulants – carrots, sliced apples, linseed.

Came the time to canter, and with some apprehension I boxed him over to the Hicksons'; but being on his own he was content to keep steady, and on the third occasion I took him right round their gallop twice, a distance of over four miles, letting him at the end spin on quite fast, but managing to stop him fairly easily just before he really got going.

The following week I gave him two sharper gallops. On the second occasion I admit that I had a job to pull him up.

I then took him over their fences. They were on the flimsy side and somewhat neglected, which was probably why he lacked his usual fluency jumping them. At the beginning of March I gave him three miles. He went well, but had less in hand at the end than I had expected, considering how much work he had done. But this, I felt, was probably due to the fact that he was galloping alone, which always takes considerably more out of a horse, and to the fact that it was still very wet at the bottom end of the gallop. Anyway there was still the tuning-up fortnight, and I was confident that Pancho would be fit to run for his life and – who knows? – win, perhaps, the coveted Lady Gordon Trophy.

It was one of those soft March days. There was no sun, but it was slightly hazy and there was a soft wind from the west; ideal for a Point-to-Point, quite different from the bitterly cold day that one so often gets.

The Members' Race is always the first on the card. There were eight runners. The handsome trophy was on view on a table at the edge of the paddock. There was a fair crowd, and it was quite a struggle to force one's way through from the weighing-tent to the paddock.

Pancho had just been led in by Sara, and after being greeted by my wife in the middle, by the number board, had started to parade round with the others. We had arranged for the box to bring Pancho as late as possible, and for him to be brought into the paddock at the last possible moment so that he had little time to get excited.

I watched him going round, looking wonderfully fit, as lithe and lean as a greyhound. I compared him with the others, and had to admit to myself that he was really in a different class, though there were some good horses

– our Members' Race always being considered the best in the neighbourhood. My opinion seemed to be shared by the public, as we were informed that the bookmakers had made him favourite. I could hear the shouting now.

'Four to one, bar! Four to one, bar!' 'Five to two, Pancho. Five to two, Pancho.' 'Threes the field!'

Pancho heard them too, and I could see he was restless. After a few minutes Sara suddenly and unexpectedly brought him into the middle.

'Do you think he's all right, Mr Garrard? He's like he was that time on Boxing Day – all shaking and sweating. Look how he's trembling.'

'It's just excitement being on a racecourse again.' I pulled his ears. They were very cold. 'He's all right,' I said, just a little doubtful. 'Keep him walking.'

Sara looked anxious. This was the first time she had led a horse round a parade ring.

'You're doing well,' I said encouragingly. 'Keep him walking.'

Another five minutes and the clerk of the course rang his bell. 'Jockeys up, please!'

I beckoned Sara. She brought him to the middle. My wife pulled his rug off. I tested his girths. I slipped off my mohair coat and waited until my wife was ready to give me a leg up.

Pancho was certainly sweating, and quivering all over. He gave a little anxious snort. I patted him. A deft lift and I was in the saddle. Suddenly in my thin colours – a lightweight jersey of royal blue with black sleeves – I felt a slight chill. But I knew that it was apprehension, partly reflecting that of my wife – I had given up point-to-pointing after Margot was born, and my wife had doubts as to whether I was really up to it now – and partly due to my anxiety for Pancho. He just had to win, or at any rate acquit himself honourably.

The huntsman, Will, one of the Hunt staff patrolling the course, blew a note on his horn, and led the way out of the paddock.

'Off we go,' I said with a rather forced lightheartedness.

'Good luck then,' my wife said quietly, lightly pressing my knee with her hand. She knew how much this race meant to me.

Sara led Pancho towards the exit. Once through she let him go.

'Do your best, Pancho,' she muttered, gulping with excitement. 'You've got to win.' And she gave him a pat.

We filed through the crowd, past the bookies, down to the course. Pancho was certainly in a great state; jigging sideways, snatching at his bit.

So much so in fact that I realized that I was going to have a proper handful taking him down to the start. More than once I had seen some wretched jockey carted all round the course, being unable to stop when reaching the start.

But that problem was delayed. We arrived at the opening on to the course, and Pancho flatly refused to go through it. I coaxed him; I urged him; I tapped him down the shoulder with my whip. But he stood there, his head up, his eyes dilated, shaking.

'Come on, silly,' I said, but I was getting anxious. People started shouting and waving behind him. That, I knew, would upset him the more. I asked them to stop, Pancho still would not move.

Out of the crowd, from nowhere, Sara suddenly

appeared. She took hold of his bridle, quietly but firmly.

'Come on, old boy.'

He hesitated for a moment or two more, then allowed himself to be led through. Once on the course he gave a great bound, and before I was properly composed he was off.

Before he had got into top gear or his head down, however, I managed to steady him; even brought him back to a half-trot, half-canter, and decided to maintain that pace all the way to the start.

Strange, I thought. Could there perhaps be something wrong?

And then at the start, contrary to all that I had feared, he stood like a statue, never moving a muscle.

The starter called out our numbers, walked across to the side of the course.

'I shall just say "Ready? Go!" and then drop the flag,' he said. 'So good luck to you.'

The other seven, who had been walking round, shortening leathers, tightening girths, exchanging badinage – I was far too occupied with my own thoughts to join in – now straightened into a line and moved forward towards the flag. I urged Pancho towards them. He responded a little reluctantly. We were still two or three lengths behind them and almost flat-footed as the starter called out: 'Ready?'

I was about to say 'Just a moment!' when he said, 'Go!' – and we were off!

As soon as Pancho saw the others gallop away from him he took hold of the bit and charged after them.

There was not a long run to the first fence, and I had Pancho steady and well in hand. I could feel the tremor through his body as he saw the fence in front of him. Less than half a dozen strides away the horse on our left, and two lengths ahead, started swerving to the right. I had to swing Pancho to make sure I would avoid him. In fact the other horse swung even more, crashed through the fence and, although he did not actually fall, deposited his jockey right in our path. I snatched Pancho up to miss him, but although this interference caused him to jump a little stickily we were safely over and away.

He was quickly into his stride, about last but one of the field. Again he jumped the next fence paukily. 'It's upset him,' I thought, and drove him on towards the open ditch. He jumped this a little better – the guardrail in front of an open ditch so often encourages boldness in a horse.

Between fences he was galloping really well, and I found that by fiddling him a little I was just able to keep him steady. He was going well within himself, which was just what I wanted. I had been afraid that he might dash off in his usual low-head-tear-away style.

But he was still anything but fluent over his fences; so unlike the way he flew them out hunting. As we approached each fence I could feel this tremor of anticipation, and then he would hesitate, losing all his momentum and shortening his stride. We must have lost at least six lengths at every fence. Between the fences he made up most of it again, but if he went on like this he would be taking too much out of himself.

We had completed three-quarters of the first circuit of the course and were just turning left-handed down to the second open ditch, which would be the third fence from home on the second circuit. It may have been the arrival at our side of the loose horse that had lost its jockey at the first fence – I don't know – but I had to drive Pancho forward to make sure that the loose horse did not cross us as we were about to take off. Suddenly Pancho took hold of the bit, swept forward, flew the open ditch like a bird, and raced on towards the straight and the next fence, which was the original first fence again.

Approaching it he properly took hold of the bit and hurled himself at it, clearing it with effortless ease and fluency. It was as though his confidence had suddenly been restored. It was as though now, suddenly he was loving it, whereas before he had been apprehensive about it, even frightened.

A cheer went up from the great crowd as a mighty leap at the next fence in the straight took us within three lengths of the leaders. By the time we reached the open ditch we had passed them, and I was aware that I was riding an outstandingly brilliant fencer.

He had settled into a rhythm by this time, and I felt it better just to sit still and let him go, rather than to interfere, trying to adjust his pace. There was a little over a mile to go and he felt as if he could last for ever. He was gaining lengths at each fence, and a quick glance round showed me that only two of the five still standing were keeping with us at all, and they were having their work cut out to do so.

The three fences across the top of the course came and went in a series of lightning, devouring strides, and I experienced a feeling of incredible exhilaration. 'He has only to stand up to win,' I thought. 'They'll never catch us now.'

We jumped the fence at the corner and turned down

towards the second open ditch, just over half a mile to go, only three more fences – and then it happened! I could mark the exact spot – I remember the very stride even. Perhaps I had instinctively half-feared it.

It was as though someone at that moment had switched off the engine. The surging, forward drive in Pancho stopped dead. He was still galloping, but with no momentum. He was just an automaton.

For a moment I thought he was injured, or wrong, that he had broken a blood-vessel. And then the truth dawned on me – it was so obvious – everything seemed to fit in. He could only stay two and a half miles – two probably, if the going was not good. I remembered the gallop at the Hicksons'. Of course – he was the two-mile chaser type, rather than the hunter-chaser type, or the National type. And two and a half miles was his limit, his absolute limit. But a Point-to-Point is three miles. All the stuffing had now gone out of him; he was cooked, he was blown; I even felt him stagger under me. Perhaps I should have pulled up, but we were still such a long way ahead. I believed that I could nurse him home.

With courage and an instinctive reflex action he was over the open ditch, and turning for the straight. Somehow he kept going – somehow he was still galloping. I nursed him, cajoled him, talked to him. There was less than half a mile to go. Perhaps if I gave him a breather he would come again. I eased him round the corner, hugging the rails, desperately trying to help him maintain his rhythm.

We were barely cantering as we approached the last but one fence. Somehow he screwed over it, almost stopped, but got going again. What courage!

It was then that I could hear the approaching hooves of one of our rivals. I glanced round. He was still some way back. I shook up Pancho again and he responded. Somehow he found a stride and drove himself on towards the last. I sat as still as I was able, giving him all the support that I could with the strength of my seat and legs, fussing him as little as possible lest I might unbalance him.

The thud of hooves came closer, but I knew that we still had enough lead to hold off that challenge; as long as we could clear the last fence – the last barrier between us and the Lady Gordon Trophy.

'You must make it, Pancho,' I breathed at him. 'Oh, Pancho, you must, you must! This will vindicate you for ever. Just one more fence. Come on, boy!'

The roar of the crowd, cheering desperately to get the favourite home, penetrated my ears – the hooves behind echoed mockingly – the last fence came closer, and closer, and closer.

Pancho laboured towards it. Only his great heart was carrying him forward. He bore relentlessly, courageously, determinedly onward. If we could meet the last fence right then I knew we would be home. But could we? He was beginning to weave slightly from left to right. I held him together with all my physical strength, forcing my knees into the saddle-flaps, every muscle in my body taut as catgut.

Six strides to go! Five! Four! Three! We were wrong. He tried to put a short one in. With all his mighty strength he attempted to lift his racked body over the last fence. But he was too close, much too close; much, much, much too close.

It was obvious that he must crash into it.

I remember no more.

I have a vague recollection of my wife gently unknotting my silk scarf. I have a blurred picture of Sara's white face and the white blaze of a horse's head haloed in steam – and big long black ears. I can still see, or more accurately smell, the antiseptic white interior of an ambulance; hear faraway voices, feel a frantic searing pain in my head.

I had fractured my skull, but it could have been worse. The first two or three days in hospital are a hazy merging of a split head, the apparently constant presence of my wife, starchy figures floating by, sometimes far, sometimes near, and an awareness of carnations.

There were increasingly lucid moments. In one of them I asked my wife: 'Is he all right?'

'Trust him,' she replied softly. 'Just got up and jogged off down the straight till he met Sara running down the course from where she had been watching by the winning post. He's all right.'

Another time I asked: 'What happened?'

'He hit the fence and turned over. He can't have risen any higher than the guard-rail.'

'Poor old chap,' I muttered.

'He was cooked. He had taken too much out of himself when he pulled right away from the others going up the hill on the second circuit.'

I was too tired to explain.

She wouldn't understand anyway. He couldn't stay more than two miles. It was only his courage that had got him to the last fence. However much he had been nursed he would never have got three miles. Never. He was not bred that way – that's what counts. Poor old chap. I ought to have pulled him up. But I had so wanted him to vindicate himself. That cup. He did his best. It had nearly come off. The spirit had been willing enough. It was no fault of his that the flesh was weak. My head was splitting. I drifted off.

Chapter Fourteen

Mr Jorrocks at Newmarket

R. S. Surtees

'A muffin – and *The Post*, sir,' said George to the Yorkshireman, on one of the fine fresh mornings that gently usher in the returning spring, and draw from the town-pent Cits sighs for the verdure of the fields – as he placed the above-mentioned articles on his usual breakfast-table in the coffee-room of the Piazza.

With the calm deliberation of a man whose whole day is unoccupied, the Yorkshireman sweetened his tea, drew the muffin and a select dish of prawns to his elbow, and turning sideways to the table, crossed his legs and prepared to con the contents of the paper. The first page as usual was full of advertisements. Sales by Auction – Favour of your Vote and Interest – If the next of Kin – Reform your Tailor's Bills – Law – Articled Clerk – An Absolute Reversion – Pony Phaeton – Artificial Teeth – Messrs Tattersall – Brace of Pointers – Dog lost – Boy Found – Great Sacrifice – No Advance in Coffee – Matrimony – A Single Gentleman – Board and Lodging in an Airy Situation – To Omnibus Proprietors – Steam to Leith and Hull – Stationery – Desirable Investment for a small Capital – The Fire Reviver or Lighter.

Then, turning it over, his eye ranged over a whole meadow of type consisting of the previous night's debate, followed on by City News, Police Reports, Fashionable Arrivals and Departures, Dinners Given, Sporting Intelligence, Newmarket Craven Meeting. 'That's more in my way,' said the Yorkshireman to himself as he laid down the paper and took a sip of his tea. 'I've a great mind to go, for I may just as well be at Newmarket as here, having nothing particular to do in either place. I came to stay £100 in London, it's true, but if I stay ten of it at Newmarket, it'll be all the same, and I can go home from there just as well as from here': so saying, he took another turn at the tea. The race list was a tempting one, Riddlesworth, Craven Stakes, Column Stakes, Oatlands, Port, Claret, Sherry, Madeira, and all other sorts. A good week's racing, in fact, for the saintly sinners who frequent the Heath had not then discovered any greater impropriety in travelling on a Sunday than in cheating each other on the Monday. The tea was good, as were the prawns and eggs, and George brought a second muffin, at the very moment that the Yorkshireman had finished the last piece of the first, so that by the time he had done his breakfast and drawn on his boots, which were drier and pleasanter than the recent damp weather had allowed of their being, he felt completely at peace with himself and all the world and putting on his hat, sallied forth with the self-satisfied air of a man who had eaten a good breakfast, and yet not too much.

Newmarket was still uppermost in his mind; and as

he sauntered along in the direction of the Strand, it occurred to him that perhaps Mr Jorrocks might have no objection to accompany him. On entering that great thoroughfare of humanity, he turned to the East, and having examined the contents of all the caricature shops in the line, and paid 3d. for a look at the York Herald, in the Chapter Coffee-house, St Paul's Churchyard, about noon he reached the corner of St Botolph-lane. Before Jorrocks and Co's warehouse, great bustle and symptoms of brisk trade were visible. With true city pride, the name on the door-post was in small dirty-white letters, sufficiently obscure to render it apparent that Mr Jorrocks considered his house required no sign; while, as a sort of contradiction, the covered errand-cart before it bore 'Jorrocks & Co's Wholesale Tea Warehouse' in great gilt letters on each side of the cover, so large that 'he who runs might read', even though the errand-cart were running too. Into this cart, which was drawn by the celebrated rat-tail hunter, they were pitching divers packages for town delivery, and a couple of light porters nearly upset the Yorkshireman, as they bustled out with their loads. The warehouse itself gave evident proof of great antiquity. It was not one of your fine, light, lofty mahogany-countered, banker-like establishments of modern times, where the stock-in-trade often consists of books and empty canisters, but a large, roomy, gloomy, dirty, dingy sort of cellar above ground, full of hogsheads, casks, flasks, sugar-loaves, jars, bags, bottles, and boxes.

The floor was half an inch thick, at least, with dirt, and was sprinkled with rice, currants, and raisins, as though they had been scattered for the purpose of growing. A small corner seemed to have been cut off, like the fold of a Leicestershire grazing ground, and made into an office, in the centre of which was a square or two of glass that commanded a view of the whole warehouse. 'Is Mr Jorrocks in?' inquired the Yorkshireman of a porter, who was busy digging currants with a wooden spade. 'Yes, sir; you'll find him in the counting-house,' was the answer; but on looking in, though his hat and gloves were there, no Jorrocks was visible. At the further end of the warehouse a man in his shirt-sleeves, with a white apron round his waist and a brown-paper cap on his head, was seen under a very melancholy-looking skylight, holding his head over something, as if his nose were bleeding. The Yorkshireman groped his way up to him, and asking if Mr Jorrocks was in, found he was addressing the grocer himself. He had been leaning over a large tray-full of little white cups – with teapots to match – trying the strength, flavour, and virtue of a large purchase of tea, and the beverage was all smoking before him. 'My vig,' exclaimed he, holding out his hand, 'who'd have thought of seeing you in the city; this is something unkimmon! However, you're werry welcome in St Botolph-lane, and as this is your first visit, why, I'll make you a present of some tea – what do you drink? black or green, or perhaps both – 4 lb. of one and 2 lb. of t'other – Here, Joe!' summoning his foreman, 'put up 4 lb. of that last lot of black that came in, and 2 lb. of superior green, and this gentleman will tell you where to leave it. – And when do you think of starting?' again addressing the Yorkshireman – 'egad, this is fine weather for the country – have half a mind to have a jaunt myself – makes one quite young – feel as if I'd laid full fifty years aside, and were again a boy – when did you say you start?' 'Why, I don't know exactly,' replied the Yorkshireman; 'the weather's so fine that I'm half tempted to go round by Newmarket.' 'Newmarket!' exclaimed Jorrocks, throwing his arm in the air, while his paper cap fell from his head with a jerk – 'by Newmarket! why, what in the name of all that's impure, have you to do at Newmarket?'

'Why, nothing in particular; only, when there's neither hunting nor shooting going on, what is a man to do with himself? – I'm sure you'd despise me if I were to go fishing.' 'True,' observed Mr Jorrocks, somewhat subdued, and jingling the silver in his breeches-pocket. 'Fox-'unting is indeed the prince of sports. The image of war without its guilt and only half its danger. I confess that I'm a martyr to it – a perfect wictim: no one knows that I suffer from my ardour. If ever I'm wisited with the last infirmity of noble minds, it will be caused by my ungovernable passion for the chase. The sight of a saddle makes me sweat. An 'ound makes me perfectly wild. A red coat throws me into a scarlet fever. Never throughout life have I had a good night's rest before an 'unting morning. But werry little racing does for me; Sadler's Wells is well enough of a fine summer evening – especially when they plump the clown over head in the New River cut, and the ponies don't misbehave in the Circus – but, oh! Newmarket's a dreadful place, the werry name's a sickener. I used to hear a vast about it from poor Will Softly, of Friday-street. It was the ruin of him – and what a fine business his father left him, both wholesale and retail, in the tripe and cowheel line – all went in two years, and he had nothing to show at the end of that time, for upwards of 20,000 golden sovereigns, but a hundredweight of children's lamb's-wool socks, and warrants for thirteen hogsheads of damaged sherry in the Docks. No, take my advice, and have nothing to say to them – stay where you are, or if you're short of swag, come to Great Coram-street, where you shall have a bed, wear-and-tear for your teeth and all that sort of thing found you, and, if Saturday's a fine day, I'll treat you with a jaunt to Margate.'

'You are a regular old trump,' said the Yorkshireman, after listening attentively until Mr Jorrocks had exhausted himself, 'but, you see, you've never been at Newmarket, and the people have been hoaxing you about it. I can assure you, from personal experience, that the people there are quite as honest as those you meet every day on "Change", besides which, there is nothing more invigorating to the human frame, nothing more cheering to the spirits, than the sight and air of Newmarket Heath on a fine fresh spring morning like the present. The wind seems to go by you at a racing pace, and the blood canters up and down the veins with the finest and freest action imaginable. A stranger to the racecourse would feel, and almost instinctively know, what turf he was treading, and the purpose for which that turf was intended.

"There's a magic in the web of it".'

'Oh, I knows you're a most persuadive cock,' observed Mr Jorrocks, interrupting the Yorkshireman, 'and would conwince the devil himself that black is white, but you'll never make me believe the Newmarket folks are honest; and as to the fine hair (air) you talk of, there's quite as good to get on Hampstead Heath, and if it doesn't make the blood canter up and down your weins, you can always amuse yourself by watching the donkeys cantering up and down with the sweet little children – haw, haw, haw! But, tell me, what is there at Newmarket that should take a man there?' 'What is there?' rejoined the Yorkshireman; 'why, there's everything that makes life desirable and constitutes happiness, in this world, except hunting. First, there is the beautiful, neat, clean town, with groups of booted professors, ready for the rapidest march of intellect; then there are the strings of clothed horses – the finest in the world – passing indolently at intervals to their exercise, the flower of English aristocracy residing in the place. You leave the town and stroll to the wide, open heath, where all is brightness and space; the white rails stand forth against the clear blue sky – the brushing gallop ever and anon startles the ear and eye; crowds of stable urchins, full of silent importance, stud the heath; you feel elated, and long to bound over the well groomed turf, and to try the speed of the careering wind. All things at Newmarket train the mind to racing. Life seems on the start, and dull indeed were he who could rein in his feelings when such inspiriting objects meet together to madden them.'

'Bravo!' exclaimed Jorrocks, throwing his paper cap in the air as the Yorkshireman concluded, 'Bravo! werry good indeed! You speak like ten Lord Mayors – never heard nothing better. Dash my vig, if I won't go. By Jove, you've done it. Tell me one thing: is there a good place to feed at?'

'Capital!' replied the Yorkshireman, 'beef, mutton, cheese, ham, all the delicacies of the season, as the sailor said;' and thereupon the Yorkshireman and Jorrocks shook hands upon the bargain.

Sunday night arrived, and with it arrived, at the Belle Sauvage, in Ludgate Hill, Mr Jorrocks's boy 'Binjimin', with Mr Jorrocks's carpet-bag; and shortly after, Mr Jorrocks, on his chestnut hunter, and the Yorkshireman, in a hack cab, entered the yard. Having consigned his horse to Binjimin, after giving him a very instructive lesson relative to the manner in which he would chastise him if he heard of his trotting or playing any tricks with the horse on his way home, Mr Jorrocks proceeded to pay the remainder of his fare in the coach-office. The mail was full inside and out! indeed, the book-keeper assured him he could have filled a dozen or more, so anxious were all London to see the Riddlesworth run. 'Inside,' said he, 'are you and your friend, and if it weren't that the night air might give you cold, Mr Jorrocks' (for all the book-keepers in London knew him), 'I should have liked to have got you outsides, and I tried to make an exchange with two blacklegs, but they would hear of nothing less than 2 gns. a head which wouldn't do, you know. Here comes another of your passengers – a great foreign nobleman, they say – Baron something – though he looks as much like a foreign pick-pocket as anything else.'

'Vich be de *voiture*?' inquired a tall, gaunt-looking foreigner, with immense moustache, a high conical hat, with a bright buckle, long, loose, bluish-blackish frock-coat, very short white waistcoat, baggy brownish striped trousers, and long-footed Wellington boots, with a sort of Chinese turn up at the toe. 'Vich be de Newmarket *voiture*?' said he, repeating the query, as he entered the office and deposited a silk umbrella, a camlet cloak, and a Swiss knapsack on the counter. The porter, without any attempt at an answer, took his goods and walked off to the mail, followed closely by the baron, and after depositing the cloak inside, so that the baron might ride with his 'face to the horses', as the saying is, he turned the knapsack into the hind boot, and swung himself into the office till it was time to ask for something for his exertions. Meanwhile the baron made a tour of the yard, taking a lesson in English from the lettering on the various coaches, when on the hind boot of one, he deciphered the word Cheapside, 'Ah, Cheapside!' said he, pulling out his dictionary, and turning to the letter C. 'Chaste, chat, chaw – cheap, dat be it. Cheap – to be had at a low price – small value. Ah! I hev (have) it,' said he, stamping and knitting his brows, '*sacré-e-e-e-e nom de Dieu,*' and the first word being drawn out to its usual longitude, three strides brought him and the conclusion of the oath into the office together. He then opened out upon the book-keeper, in a tremendous volley of French, English, and Hanoverian, oaths, for he was a cross between the first and last named countries, the purport of which was 'dat he had paid de best price, and he be dem if he vod ride on de cheap side of de coach.' In vain the clerks and book-keepers tried to convince him he was wrong in his interpretation. With the full conviction of a foreigner that he was about to be cheated, he had his cloak shifted to the opposite side of the coach, and the knapsack placed on the roof. The fourth inside having cast up, the outside passengers mounted, the insides took their places, threepences and sixpences were pulled out for the porters, the guard twanged his horn, the coachman turned out his elbow, flourished his whip, caught the point, cried 'All right! sit tight!' and trotted out of the yard.

Jorrocks and the Yorkshireman sat opposite each other, the Baron and Old Sam Spring, the betting man, did likewise. Who doesn't know old Sam, with his curious tortoiseshell rimmed spectacles, his old drab hat turned up with green, careless neckcloth, flowing robe, and comical cut? He knew Jorrocks – though – tell it not in Coram-street, he didn't know his name; but concluding from the disparity of age between him and his companion, that Jorrocks was either a shark or a shark's jackal, and the Yorkshireman a victim, with due professional delicacy he contented himself with scrutinizing the latter through his specs. The Baron's choler having subsided, he was the first to break the ice of silence. 'Foine noight,' was the observation, which was thrown out promiscuously to see who would take it up. Now Sam Spring, though he came late, had learned from the porter that there was a baron in the coach, and being a great admirer of the nobility, for whose use he has a code of signals of his own, consisting of one finger to his hat for a Baron Lord, as he calls them, two for a Viscount, three for a Duke, he immediately responded with 'Yes, my lord,' with a forefinger to his hat. There is something sweet in the word 'Lord' which finds its way home to the heart of an Englishman. No sooner did Sam pronounce it, than the baron became transformed in Jorrocks's eyes into a very superior sort of person, and forthwith he commenced ingratiating himself by offering him a share of a large paper of sandwiches, which the baron accepted with the greatest condescension, eating what he could and stuffing the remainder into his hat. His lordship was a better hand at eating than speaking, and the united efforts of the party could not extract from him the precise purport of his journey. Sam threw out two or three feasible offers in the way of bets, but they fell still-born to the bottom of the coach, and Jorrocks talked to him about hunting and had the conversation all to himself, the baron merely replying with a bow and a stare, sometimes diversified with, 'I tank you – vare good.' The conversation by degrees resolved itself into a snore, in which they were all indulging, when the raw morning air rushed in among them, as a porter with lanthorn opened the door and announced their arrival at Newmarket. Forthwith they turned into the street, and, the outside passengers having descended, they all commenced straddling, yawning, and stretching their limbs, while the guard and porters assorted their luggage. The Yorkshireman, having an eye to a bed, speedily had Mr Jorrocks's luggage and his own on the back of a porter on its way to the Rutland Arms, while that worthy citizen followed in a sort of sleepy astonishment at the smallness of the place, inquiring if they were sure they had not stopped at some village by mistake. Two beds had been ordered for two gentlemen who could not get two seats by the mail, which fell to the lot of those who did, and into these our heroes trundled, having arranged to be called by the early exercising hour.

Whether it was from want of his usual nightcap of brandy-and-water, or the fatigues of travelling, or what else, remains unknown, but no sooner was Mr Jorrocks left alone with his candle, than all at once he was seized with a sudden fit of trepidation, on thinking that he should have been inveigled to such a place as Newmarket, and the tremor increasing as he pulled four £5 bank-notes out of his watch-pocket, besides a vast quantity of silver and his great gold watch, he was resolved, should an attempt be made upon his property, to defend it with his life, and having squeezed the notes into the toe of his boots, and hid the silver in the wash-hand stand, he very deliberately put his watch and the poker under the pillow, and set the heavy chest of drawers with two stout chairs and a table against the door, after all which exertions he got into bed and very soon fell sound asleep.

Most of the inmates of the house were up with the lark to the early exercise, and the Yorkshireman was as early as any of them. Having found Mr Jorrocks's door, he commenced a loud battery against it without awaking the grocer; he then tried to open it, but only succeeded in getting it an inch or two from the post, and after several holloas of 'Jorrocks, my man! Mr Jorrocks! Jorrocks, old boy! holloa, Jorrocks!' he succeeded in extracting the word 'Wot?' from the worthy gentleman as he rolled over in his bed. 'Jorrocks!' repeated the Yorkshireman, 'it's time to be up.' 'Wot?' again was the answer. 'Time to get up. The morning's breaking.' 'Let it break,' replied he, adding in a mutter, as he turned over again, 'it owes me nothing.'

Entreaties being useless, and a large party being on the point of setting off, the Yorkshireman joined them, and spent a couple of hours on the dew-bespangled heath, during which time they not only criticized the figure and action of every horse that was out, but got up tremendous appetites for breakfast. In the meantime Mr Jorrocks had risen, and having attired himself with his usual care, in a smart blue coat with metal buttons, buff waistcoat, blue stocking-netted tights, and Hessian boots, he turned into the main street of Newmarket, where he was lost in astonishment at the insignificance of the place. But wiser men than Mr Jorrocks have been similarly disappointed, for it enters into the philosophy of few to conceive the fame and grandeur of Newmarket compressed into the limits of the petty, outlandish, Icelandish place that bears the name. 'Dash my vig,' said Mr Jorrocks as he brought himself to bear upon Rogers's shop-window, 'this is the werry meanest town I ever did see. Pray, sir,' addressing himself to a groomish-looking man in a brown cut-away coat, drab shorts and continuations, who had just emerged from the shop with a race list in his hand – 'pray, sir, be this your principal street?' The man eyed him with a mixed look of incredulity and contempt. At length, putting his thumbs into the armholes of his waistcoat, he replied, 'I bet a crown you know as well as I do.' 'Done,' said Mr Jorrocks, holding out his hand. 'No – I won't do that,' replied the man, 'but I'll tell you what I'll do with you – I'll lay you 2 to 1, in fives or fifties if you like, that you knew before you axed, and that Thunderbolt don't win the Riddlesworth.' 'Really,' said Mr Jorrocks, 'I'm not a betting man.' 'Then, wot the 'ell business have you at Newmarket?' was all the answer he got. Disgusted with such inhospitable impertinence, Mr Jorrocks turned on his heel and walked away. Before the White Hart Inn was a smartish pony phaeton, in charge of a stunted stable lad. 'I say, young chap,' inquired Jorrocks, 'whose is that?' 'How did you know that I was a young chap?' inquired the abortion, turning round. 'Guessed it,' replied Jorrocks, chuckling at his own wit. 'Then guess whose it is.'

'Pray are your clocks here by London time?' he asked of a respectable elderly-looking man whom he saw turn out of the entry leading to the Kingston rooms, and take the usual survey first up the town and then down it, and afterwards compose his hands in his breeches-pockets, there to stand to see the 'world'.* 'Come now, old'un – none o' your tricks here – you've got a match on against time, I suppose,' was all the answer he could get, after the man (old R—n the ex-flagellator) had surveyed him from head to foot.

We need hardly say after all these rebuffs that when Mr Jorrocks met the Yorkshireman, he was not in the best possible humour; indeed, to say nothing of the extreme sharpness and suspicion of the people, we know of no place where a man, not fond of racing, is so completely out of his element as at Newmarket; for with the exception of a little 'elbow-shaking' in the evening, there is literally and truly nothing else to do.

It is 'Heath,' 'Ditch in,' 'Abingdon mile,' 'T.Y.C. Stakes,' 'Sweepstakes,' 'Handicaps,' 'Bet,' 'Lay,' 'Take,' 'Odds,' 'Evens,' morning, noon, and night.

Mr Jorrocks made bitter complaints during the breakfast, and some invidious comparisons between racing men and fox-hunters, which, however, became softer towards the close, as he got deeper in the delicacy of a fine Cambridge brawn. Nature being at length appeased, he again thought of turning out, to have a look, as he said, at the shows on the course, but the appearance of his friend the Baron opposite the window put it out of his head, and he sallied forth to join him. The Baron was evidently incog.; for he had on the same short dirty-white waistcoat, Chinese boots, and conical hat, that he had travelled down in, and being a stranger in the land of course he was uncommonly glad to pick up Jorrocks; so after he had hugged him a little, called him a '*bon garçon*', and a few other endearing terms, he

* Newmarket or London – it's all the same – 'The World' is but composed of one's own acquaintance.

ran his great long arm through his and walked him down street, the whole peregrinations of Newmarket being comprised in the words ‘up street’ and ‘down’. He then communicated, in most unrepresentable language, that he was on his way to buy ‘an ’oss’, and Jorrocks informing him that he was a perfect connoisseur in the article, the Baron again assured him of his distinguished consideration. They were met by Joe Rogers, the trainer, with a ring key in his hand, who led the way to the stable, and having unlocked a box in which was a fine slapping 4-year-old, according to etiquette, he put his hat in a corner, took a switch in one hand, laid hold of the horse’s head with the other, while the lad in attendance stripped off its clothes. The Baron then turned up his wrists, and making a curious noise in his throat, proceeded to pass his hand down each leg, and along its back, after which he gave it a thump in the belly and squeezed its throat, when, being as wise as he was at starting, he stuck his thumb in his side, and took a mental survey of the whole – ‘Ah,’ said he at length – ‘foin ’oss; vot ears he has?’ ‘Oh,’ said Rogers, ‘they show breeding.’ ‘*Non*, *non*, I say vot ears he has?’ ‘Well, but he carries them well,’ was the answer. ‘*Non non*,’ stamping, ‘I say vot ears (years) he has?’ ‘Oh, hang it, I twig – 4 years old.’ Then the Baron took another long look at him. At length he resumed, ‘I vill my wet.’ ‘What’s that?’ inquired Rogers of Jorrocks. ‘His wet – why, a drink to be sure,’ and thereupon Rogers went to the pump and brought a glass of pure water, which the Baron refused with becoming indignation. ‘*Non*, *non*,’ said he, stamping, ‘I vill my wet,’ repeated the Baron with vehemence. ‘He must want some brandy in it,’ observed Mr Jorrocks, judging of the Baron by himself, and thereupon the lad was sent for three-penn'orth. When it arrived, the Baron dashed it out of his hand with a prolonged *sacré-e-e-e*! adding, 'I vill vont wet-tin-nin-na-ary surgeon.' The boy was despatched for one, and on his arrival the veterinary surgeon went through the process the Baron had attempted, and not being a man of many words, he just gave the Baron a nod at the end. 'How moch?' inquired the Baron of Rogers. 'Five hundred,' was the answer. 'Vot, 500 *livre*?' 'Oh d—n it, you may take him or leave him, just as you like, but you won't get him for less.' The 'vet' explained that the Baron wished to know whether it was 500 francs (French tenpences), or 500 gns. English money, and being informed that it was the latter, he gave his conical hat a thrust on his brow, and bolted out of the box.

But race hour approaches, and people begin to assemble in groups before the 'rooms', while tax-carts, pony-gigs, post-chaises, the usual aristocratical accompaniments of Newmarket, come dribbling at intervals into the town. Here is old Sam Spring, in a spring cart, driven by a plough-boy in fustian; there is the Earl of —, on a £10 pony, with the girths elegantly parted to prevent the saddle slipping over its head; while Miss —, his jockey's daughter, dashes by him in a phaeton, with a powdered footman, and the postillion in scarlet and leathers, with a badge on his arm. Old Crockey puts on his great-coat, Jem Bland draws the yellow phaeton and greys to the gateway of the White Hart, to take up his friend Crutch Robinson; Zac, Jack, and another have just driven on in a fly. In short, it's a brilliant meeting! Besides four coronetted carriages with post horses, there are three phaetons-and-pair; a thing that would have been a phaeton if they'd have let it, General Grosvenor's dog-carriage – that is to say, his carriage with a dog upon it; Lady Chesterfield and the Hon. Mrs Anson in a pony-phaeton with an outrider (Miss — will have one next meeting instead of the powdered footman); Tattersall in his double carriage, driving without bearing-reins; Old Theobald in leather breeches and a buggy; five Bury butchers in a tax-cart; Young Dutch Sam on a pony; 'Short-odds Richards' on a long-backed, crocodile-looking Rosinante; and no end of pedestrians.

But where is Mr Jorrocks all this time? Why, eating brawn in the Rutland Arms with his friend the Baron, perfectly unconscious that all these passers-by were not the daily visibles of the place. 'Dash my vig,' said he, as he bolted another half of the round, 'I see no symptoms of a stir. Come, my lord, do me the honour to take another glass of sherry.' His lordship was nothing loath, so by mutual entreaties they finished the bottle, besides a considerable quantity of port. A fine, fat, chestnut, long-tailed Suffolk-Punch cart mare – fresh from the plough – having been considerately provided by the Yorkshireman for Mr Jorrocks, with a cob for himself, they proceeded to mount in the yard, when Mr Jorrocks was concerned to find that the Baron had nothing to carry him. His lordship, too, seemed disconcerted, but it was only momentarily; for walking up to the Punch mare, and resting his elbow on her hind quarter to try if she kicked, he very coolly vaulted up behind Mr Jorrocks. Now Jorrocks, though proud of the patronage of a lord, did not exactly comprehend whether he was in earnest or not; but the Baron soon let him know, for, thrusting his conical hat on his brow, he put his arm round Jorrocks's waist, and gave the old mare a touch in the flank with the Chinese boot, crying out, 'Along me, *brave garçon*, along, *ma chère*!' and, the owner of the mare living at Kentford, she went off at a brisk trot in that direction, while the Yorkshireman slipped down the town unperceived. The sherry had done its business on them both; the Baron, who, perhaps, was the most 'cut' of the two, chanted the Marseillaise hymn of liberty, with as much freedom as though he were sitting in the saddle. Thus they proceeded, laughing and singing, until the Bury pay-gate arrested their progress, when it occurred to the steersman to ask if they were going right. 'Be this the vay to Newmarket races?' inquired Jorrocks of the pike-keeper. The man dived into the small pocket of his white apron for a ticket, and very coolly replied, 'Shell out, old 'un.' 'How much?' said Jorrocks. 'Tuppence,' which having got, he said, 'Now then, you may turn, for the heath be over yonder,' pointing back; 'at least, it was there this morning, I know.' After a volley of abuse for his impudence, Mr Jorrocks, with some difficulty, got the mare pulled round, for she had a deuced hard mouth of her own, and only a plain snaffle in it. At last, however, with the aid of a boy to beat her with a furze bush, they got her set a-going again, and, retracing their steps, they trotted 'down street', rose the hill and entered the spacious, wide-extending flat of Newmarket Heath. The races were going forward on one of the distant courses, and a slight, insignificant black streak, swelling into a sort of oblong (for all the world like an overgrown tadpole), was all that denoted the spot, or interrupted the verdant aspect of the quiet extensive plain. Jorrocks was horrified, having through life pictured Epsom as a mere drop in the ocean compared with the countless multitude of Newmarket, while the Baron, who was wholly indifferent to the matter, nearly had old Jorrocks pitched over the mare's head by applying the furze bush, which he had got from the boy, to her tail, while Mr Jorrocks was sitting loosely, contemplating the barrenness of the prospect. The sherry was still alive, and, being all for fun, he shuffled back into the saddle as soon as the old mare gave over kicking; and, giving a loud tally-ho, with some minor 'hunting noises', which were responded to by the Baron in notes not capable of being set to music, and aided by an equally indescribable accompaniment from the old mare at every application of the bush, she went off at score over the springy turf, and bore them triumphantly to the betting post, just as the ring was in course of formation, a fact which she announced by a loud neigh on viewing her companion of the plough, as well as by upsetting some half-dozen blacklegs, as she rushed through the crowd to greet her. Great was the hubbub, shouting, swearing, and laughing; for, though the Newmarketites are familiar with most conveyances, from a pair of horses down to a pair of shoes, it had not then fallen to their lot to see two men ride into the ring on the same horse – certainly not with such a hat between them as the Baron's.

The gravest and weightiest matters will not long distract the attention of a blackleg, and the laughter having subsided without Jorrocks or the Baron being in the slightest degree disconcerted, the ring was again formed; horses' heads again turned towards the post, while carriages, gigs, and carts form an outer circle. A solemn silence ensues. The legs are scanning the list. At length one gives tongue. 'What starts? Does Lord Eldon start?' 'No, he don't,' replies the owner. 'Does Trick by Catton?' 'Yes, and Conolly rides – but mind, 3 lb. over.' 'Does John Bull?' 'No, John's struck out.' 'Polly Hopkins does, so does Talleyrand, also O, Fy! out of Penitence. Beagle and Paradox also – and perhaps Pickpocket.'

Another pause and the pencils are pulled from the betting-books. The legs and lords look at each other, but no one likes to lead off. At length a voice is heard offering to take 9 to 1 he names the winner. 'It's short odds, doing it cautiously.' 'I'll take eight then,' he adds – 'sivin!' but no one bites. 'What will anyone lay about Trick, by Catton?' inquires Jem Bland. 'I'll lay 3 to 1 against him.' 'I'll take 2 to 1 – two ponies to one, and give you a suv for laying it.' 'Carn't,' is the answer. 'I'll do it, Jem, 'cries a voice. 'No, you won't,' from Bland, not liking his customer. Now they are all at it, and what a hubbub there is! 'I'll back the field – I'll lay – I'll take – I'll bet – ponies – fifties – hundreds – 500 to 2.' 'What do you want, my lord?' '3 to 1 against Trick by Catton.' 'Can't afford it – the odds really aren't that in the ring. Take two – 200 to 1.' 'No. Crockford, you'll do it for me?' 'Yes, my lord. Twice over, if you like. Done, done.' 'Do it again?' 'No, thank you.'

'Trick, by Catton, don't start!' cries a voice. 'Impossible!' exclaim his backers. 'Quite true, I'm just from the weighing-house, and — told me so himself.' 'Shame! shame!' roar those who have backed him, and 'honour – rascals – rogues – thieves – robbery – swindle – turf-ruined' fly from tongue to tongue, but they are all speakers with never a speaker to cry order. Meanwhile the lads have galloped by on their hacks with the horses' clothes to the rubbing-house, and the horses have actually started, and are now visible in the distance sweeping over the open heath, apparently without guide or beacon.

The majority of the ring rush to the white judge's box, and have just time to range themselves along the rude stakes and ropes that guard the run-in, and the course-keeper in a shooting jacket on a rough pony to crack his whip, and cry to half-a-dozen stable lads to 'clear the course', before the horses come flying towards home. Now all is tremor; hope and fear vacillating in each breast. Silence stands breathless with expectation – all eyes are riveted – the horses come within descrying distance – 'beautiful!' three close together, two behind. 'Clear the course! clear the course! pray clear the course!' 'Polly Hopkins! Polly Hopkins!' roar a hundred voices as they near; 'O, Fy! O, Fy!' respond an equal number. 'The horse! the horse!' bellow a hundred more, as though their yells would aid his speed, as Polly Hopkins, O, Fy! and Talleyrand rush neck and neck along the cords and pass the judge's box. A cry of 'dead heat!' is heard. The bystanders see as suits their books, and immediately rush to the judge's box, betting, bellowing, roaring, and yelling the whole way. 'What's won? what's won? what's won?' is vociferated from a hundred voices. 'Polly Hopkins! Polly Hopkins! Polly Hopkins!' replies Mr Clark, with judicial dignity. 'By how much? by how much?' 'Half a head – half a head,'* replies the same functionary. 'What's second?' 'O, Fy!', and so, amid the song of 'Pretty, pretty Polly Hopkins,' from the winners, and

* No judge ever gave a race as won by half a head; but we let the whole passage stand as originally written – *Editor*.

curses and execrations, long, loud and deep, from the losers, the scene closes.

The admiring winners follow Polly to the rubbing-house, while the losing horses are left in the care of their trainers and stable-boys, who console themselves with hopes of 'better luck next time'.

Chapter Fifteen

The Haunted Hunt

R. J. Richardson

It was the middle of February that Nunn was killed, and a fortnight after his funeral we hunted again, the first whipper-in carrying the horn under a temporary committee for a couple of months.

Next season Furlong, from the Burstover, took the Mastership, bringing his own whipper-in and huntsman. The huntsman was one of the slow 'tryback' family coachman sort and although, thanks to a succession of good scenting days in the early part of the season, we had fair sport, the proceedings seemed very dull after Nunn's brilliance. Furlong brought a few hounds of his own but took over the greater part of Nunn's pack, and even these seemed affected by the changed spirit of things. Old Marksman, in particular, was not the same animal; from being the oracle of the pack he became a mute, listless slinker. So markedly so, that Furlong thought of putting him down, and the huntsman remarked with a grin, 'So this is the famous Marksman!'

The hounds had not been to Canoby Whin at all that season until one day, late in December, nearly a year after Nunn's death, when they met at the Black Bowl which is a very few miles from there. There was no scent in the morning, and we had done nothing but potter about until we came to the Whin late in the afternoon. There I got my second horse, a brown 5-year-old thoroughbred called Pride of Tyrone, which I had bought out of Ireland for a larger price than I could really afford, but which I confidently expected to recover, with interest, as a steeple-chaser. I even cherished golden dreams of future Grand Nationals. My young horse was rather a handful in a crowd, so I went on to the whipper-in at the far end of the covert. We had not long to wait before there was a whimper and half-a-minute later, there, stealing away, was my old acquaintance the big grey bob-tailed dog fox. Away he went on his familar line. I, with the thoughtlessness of youth, and in the excitement of getting away with the hounds, never noticed that I was riding at the very part of the bank which had been fatal to Anthony Nunn. I was coming nicely at it when suddenly, without any apparent reason, Pride of Tyrone swerved, crossed his legs and fell, shooting me out of the saddle, but quite unhurt I picked myself up at once. The horse was already on his feet some yards away, drenched with sweat and plunging back towards Whin. As I started to go after him he circled round at a canter and went at the bank exactly as if he had been ridden at it. I was too late to intercept him. He popped on and off like a bird, and strode away over the rise of the next field. I remember noticing, as he went past me, that the reins had somehow got caught on the saddle.

By this time the field were galloping by me, some going over the bank as the shortest way, others following the huntsman through a gap a hundred yards or more to the left. Running across the field and climbing on to the next bank for a better view, I could see the hounds fairly racing. Close up with them, served by his great speed, was the runaway Pride of Tyrone; a widening space between them and the rapidly trailing field.

Pursuit on foot was out of the question. There was no probability of anyone stopping him, and my anxiety was great lest he should manage to injure himself. I was at my wits' end what to do until it occurred to me that my first horse might still be within hail. I ran back as fast as I could, across the two fields and on to the road at the top of the Whin, where I came upon a group of second horsemen just turning away from watching the disappearing hounds, and among them was my man. Fortunately, we had done nothing to speak of before I changed on to Pride of Tyrone, so the horse was quite fresh and I galloped off in pursuit of the fugitive.

The hounds and Pride of Tyrone and all were out of sight and earshot by this time, but the tracks of the horse led straight away over the line the grey fox knew so well. It was not long before I began to meet people coming back, thrown out by falling or beaten by the pace, among them the first whipper-in with his horse badly staked. But of Pride of Tyrone there was no sign, and the tale of the casualties did not tend to lessen my uneasiness on his account.

The tracks became fewer and fewer and at length, between Humbley Farm and Buckfield, I encountered a man leading his horse back. From him I learnt that the pace, terrific for the first few miles, had slackened to a slow, hunting run when he, alone of all the field anywhere within sight of the hounds, had come to grief. He said that when he had last seen the hounds they were running straight ahead, more slowly, but in full cry, and right up alongside them, moving like a machine as though he revelled in the game, was my embryo racehorse. Wasting no time, I followed Pride of Tyrone's trail. For the greater part of the way it was plain enough and I was able to travel at a good pace, but in places, especially on the downs and higher lying grass lands, it was only with the greatest difficulty that I could find anything to guide me at all. The tracks went straight over Restland Park and Shepley Down to just below Hindholt, where the fox had evidently been headed and swung left-handed along Kelton Bottom. I saw the tracks of the hounds in the soft ground there and I knew that Pride of Tyrone was still with them.

Coming up to Checkley, on to the high land again, the line lay right over Anyman's Down to Cockover Wood, where the hoof marks were a puzzle that took me some time to unravel. From what I could make of them Pride of Tyrone had galloped into the wood, had turned halfway down the ride, had walked and trotted back, standing still more than once and had broken into a gallop again before leaving the wood by the way he had entered it, going away in the direction of Swingstone. In another hour or so it would be too dark to see any track at all. I seemed to be no nearer to Pride of Tyrone than when I started and my chance of catching him before nightfall seemed remote in the extreme, but I was determined to persevere while I could and kept plodding along the trail. From Swingstone it led right, on by High Trees and Kyte Common, as straight as a die past Ridgewater Hill and on to the Teal Valley. Sinking the valley, I followed it through Frogbere plantation and across the water meadows straight to Teal. Surely, I thought, the water would stop him, but no, I saw the marks where he had taken off. What a horse, I thought, what a horse! The Teal at that part was 30 ft. across. I knew the horse I was riding could not jump it, so, going round by the bridge a mile higher up in the village, I came along the opposite bank till I found the tracks again. As the valley was already in twilight this was no easy matter, but I struck them at last and found that Pride of Tyrone had landed, with a yard to spare, and gone straight on without hesitating. What puzzled me so much was why on earth the horse kept on and on and never hesitated or seemed to stop for a moment? By this time, my horse had had quite enough of it and as I had more and more difficulty every minute in tracking my way along, I came to the conclusion that further pursuit was hopeless.

I was just turning my head in the direction of home when the sound of hoof on the road caught my ear. I rode quickly towards the sound, and sitting on his horse in the lane which leads up to the valley by the edge of Bairn's Wood came upon the new huntsman listening intently with his hand behind his ear. Though how he, who never jumped a stick if he could help it and almost a stranger in the country, had managed to get so far I could not imagine. Certainly he had a marvellous way of picking his way about by lanes and gates and this was the only direction in which I ever knew him to exhibit the least intelligence. 'Hark!' he said, when he caught sight of me, 'Hark, they're up there,' and pointed up to where Bairn's Wood, lying on the top of the valley-side, loomed against the sunset sky. I stopped my horse and listened, but the bell-ringers were practising in Frogbere Church and the sound echoing from both sides of the valley lent itself to any construction one liked to put upon it. 'They're in there,' said the huntsman, 'I heard them before the bells began, and there's someone hunting them, too.' Someone hunting them; at this piece of information the notion flashed across me that I had come all this way on a wild goose chase. What more likely than that someone had nicked in with them, probably when the hounds had swung out of Checkley and back to Cockover Wood. I was convinced that I had been following a single line of tracks and those belonged to Pride of Tyrone, 'but,' I said to myself, 'I am not a Red Indian and it is quite possible that I have made a mistake somewhere, in spite of all my care.' After all, was it probable that any horse, least of all a young one who had that season seen hounds for the first time, would, of his own free will and riderless, stick to them all through a run like that, jumping everything as it came and the Teal as well. The more I reasoned, the more absurd did the idea seem.

As we sat there straining our ears, a labourer came down the lane from the direction of the wood. 'The hounds,' he said, in answer to our query, 'Yes, they have been up there hunting about the woods this last half-hour. Yes, there is someone with them, I heard him, no, I did not see him; I saw some of the dogs and there is a horse that has lost its master.' We rode up the lane and turned into the wood. 'Now,' said the infuriated huntsman, 'We shall see who is meddling with my hounds.' We had gone some way along the main ride before we heard hounds running towards us from the left. They came nearer and nearer and presently burst out of the undergrowth towards us from the left, and went straight up the ride in full cry. Just as they passed a branch ride leading from the left a horse darted out of it and followed in their wake. It was Pride of Tyrone in full career.

Both our horses were dead beat, so bucket along as we might we could not keep the hounds in view. The cry was getting fainter and fainter when the huntsman's horse behind me came down with a squelch and a clatter. I never stopped. I am afraid I set more value on Pride of Tyrone, and sent my horse along for all he was worth to the end of the wood. There I found that the hounds had crossed the road and gone in Oxlow Wood, with Pride of Tyrone still with them. As you know, Oxlow Wood is an irregular crescent in shape, with only one ride down the length of it. A horse can only get in or out at the ends or horns of the crescent. So, having made sure that Pride of Tyrone had entered, I cut across the far end, thinking to intercept him. There were no tracks leading out of the wood and the chances were against his turning back, so I awaited developments. The sun was just setting blood red, the sky was like a sheet of flame. Not a breath of wind stirred the woods, and behind them the mist began to creep out of the Teal Valley. The bells of Frogbere Church were still faintly audible, mingling with the intermittent cry of the hounds, which, now on one side of the wood and now on the other, were gradually coming towards me. At length the cry ceased altogether and then from the woods came a sound that made my spine crawl. It was a voice. A voice that never had a like, the voice of Anthony Nunn. 'Ye'ut,' it went, 'Ye'ut, there m'lad.' With the cold sweat dripping off me, I sat there paralysed; and the beautiful voice came on. Nearer and nearer it came, ringing and echoing through the woods like a bell.

And still I sat there, my limbs were lead and my brain numb. I sat there waiting for what unspeakable apparition I had no conception. Louder and louder it grew. 'Ye-up. Push him up. Yooi me lads. Yeu try in there.'

Then from the woods crept the dim dark form of the grey bob-tailed fox. With one foot raised, he stood listening a moment and stole away towards the sunset. In covert a hound spoke a deep note like an otter hound. 'Huick! Huick! Huick! Huick, Marksman, Huick, Huick.' The old hound crashed through the brushwood alert and eager – the Marksman of yore, throwing that sonorous tongue of his, with his nose on the line as he drove along. Dashing to his cry, the hounds poured out of the covert, and then, every muscle on my body literally twitching, I heard the voice close at hand, and an approaching horse. It seemed hours that I stared, with aching eyes that dared not blink, at the end of the ride where things must happen. What I saw burnt into my brain. Out of the wood came Pride of Tyrone! Pride of Tyrone, white with lather, eyes wild and nostrils extended. The bit pressing into his mouth: the reins extended stiffly back from the bit to an empty air about the withers. They were held in a grasp and they were held by – nothing! And from the empty air above the saddle, from on a level with my own head, pealed and cheered that clarion voice. Pride of Tyrone passed close by me. I could have touched him with my hand, and as he passed some sense of unutterable nameless horror and doom swept over me; and the voice blared like a trumpet right in my ear. 'Forrard Aw-ay.'

Blind with terror, I drove my spurs into my horse and rode away. My recollection of the journey home is a blurred jumble of furious galloping and weary leading of an exhausted horse. Next morning I went to the kennels. I found the huntsman scared and shaken, big with the news. After his fall, his horse was dead lame and as he could not hear a sound of the hounds he went home. It was after 9 o'clock when he got back to the kennels; the whipper-ins were already there, having collected four-and-half couple of the eighteen couple taken out in the morning. These four-and-half couple were all new hounds that Furlong had brought with him when he came into the country. He got his supper and went to bed. He had been asleep some time when he was aroused by violent knocking at the door. He looked out; in the yard, which was as bright as day with a brilliant moon, stood six couple of hounds. Not a sign of anything else. He was about to call out when such a feeling of horror came over him as he had not words to describe. Something was hurled past his head into the house, and out of nothing, right in the face, rang yells and shrieks of unearthly laughter. How he ever managed to bang the door to, and how long he crouched there sick with fright, he had no idea. He left the hounds outside to shift for themselves until morning. He showed me the object thrown through the door. Still lying where it had fallen was the mangled, wolfish mask of a grey dog fox, and crammed into the mouth were the four pads and a grey fragment of a brush.

During the next few days tidings came in. Pride of Tyrone was found, stiff and dead, in a lonely by-road within five miles of the kennels. Singly and in twos the rest of the hounds came back, led, in carts, and limping along on weary bleeding feet. By the end of the week there was only one hound unaccounted for. Then we had the story of the doctor of Stoatswold, in the heart of the Oaklands country. Driving home late on the night of the run, he had heard hounds breaking up a fox on the moor above the village, and someone whooping and whooping until the whole countryside resounded. The doctor said it was gruesome and turned him cold. The villagers heard it, broad awake, and shivered in their beds. Next day on the moor, by the remains of a fragment of a fox, they found a hound, dead. It was old Marksman. They must have run nearly forty miles.

Nothing of a like nature ever occurred again. For years there were rumours among the country people of a deep-voiced hound being heard at night, particularly in one part, and of a man's voice cheering him. But the evidence was never at first hand. Yet it is strange that we never find a fox in Canoby Whin.

More Beaver Books

We hope you have enjoyed this Beaver Book. Here are some of the other titles:

The Beaver Horse and Pony Quiz Book A Beaver original. See how much you know about horses and ponies by trying out some of the hundreds of questions on feeding, grooming and stable management, breeds, colours and markings, riding, showing and jumping in this book. Written by Sandy Ransford and illustrated by Christine Bousfield

Ponies in the Park A Beaver original. When a town family is left a derelict farm and decide to turn it into an animal centre, with different breeds of ponies and other animals, they encounter all kinds of problems. A thoroughly enjoyable story which will appeal to all animal lovers, written by Christine Pullein-Thompson and illustrated by Tony Morris

The Young Rider A must for all readers who love horses and ponies, this book explains all the basic principles of horsemastership – from choosing and buying a pony to caring for it and riding it. Written by Robert Owen and John Bullock, *The Young Rider* is illustrated throughout with line drawings

These and many other Beavers are available from your local bookshop or newsagent, or can be ordered direct from: Hamlyn Paperback Cash Sales, PO Box 11, Falmouth, Cornwall TR10 9EN. Send a cheque or postal order made payable to the Hamlyn Publishing Group, for the price of the book plus postage at the following rates:
UK: 45p for the first book, 20p for the second book, and 14p for each additional book ordered to a maximum charge of £1.63;
BFPO and Eire: 45p for the first book, 20p for the second book, plus 14p per copy for the next 7 books and thereafter 8p per book;
OVERSEAS: 75p for the first book and 21p for each extra book.

New Beavers are published every month and if you would like the *Beaver Bulletin*, a newsletter which tells you about new books and gives a complete list of titles and prices, send a large stamped addressed envelope to:

Beaver Bulletin
The Hamlyn Group
Astronaut House
Feltham
Middlesex TW14 9AR

362329